Tempo
A Rowman & Littlefield Music Series on Rock, Pop, and Culture
Series Editor: Scott Calhoun

Tempo: A Rowman & Littlefield Music Series on Rock, Pop, and Culture offers titles that explore rock and popular music through the lens of social and cultural history, revealing the dynamic relationship between musicians, music, and their milieu. Like other major art forms, rock and pop music comment on their cultural, political, and even economic situation, reflecting the technological advances, psychological concerns, religious feelings, and artistic trends of their times. Contributions to the **Tempo** series are the ideal introduction to major pop and rock artists and genres.

The American Songbook: Music for the Masses, by Ann van der Merwe
Billy Joel: America's Piano Man, by Joshua S. Duchan
Bob Dylan: American Troubadour, by Donald Brown
Bon Jovi: America's Ultimate Band, by Margaret Olson
British Invasion: The Crosscurrents of Musical Influence, by Simon Philo
Bruce Springsteen: American Poet and Prophet, by Donald L. Deardorff II
The Clash: The Only Band That Mattered, by Sean Egan
Glam Rock: Music in Sound and Vision, by Simon Philo
The Kinks: A Thoroughly English Phenomenon, by Carey Fleiner
Kris Kristofferson: Country Highwayman, by Mary G. Hurd
Phil Spector: The Sound of the Sixties, by Sean MacLeod
Sex Pistols: The Pride of Punk, by Peter Smith
Patti Smith: America's Punk Rock Rhapsodist, by Eric Wendell
Paul Simon: An American Tune, by Cornel Bonca
Ska: The Rhythm of Liberation, by Heather Augustyn
Sting and The Police: Walking in Their Footsteps, Aaron J. West
U2: Rock 'n' Roll to Change the World, by Timothy D. Neufeld
Warren Zevon: Desperado of Los Angeles, by George Plasketes

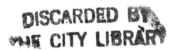

SEX PISTOLS

The Pride of Punk

Peter Smith

ROWMAN & LITTLEFIELD
Lanham • Boulder • New York • London

Published by Rowman & Littlefield
An imprint of The Rowman & Littlefield Publishing Group, Inc.
4501 Forbes Boulevard, Suite 200, Lanham, Maryland 20706
www.rowman.com

10 Thornbury Road, Plymouth PL6 7PP, United Kingdom

16 Carlisle Street, London W1D 3BT, United Kingdom

British Library Cataloguing in Publication Information Available

Library of Congress Cataloging-in-Publication Data

Names: Smith, Peter, 1956– author.
Title: Sex Pistols : the pride of punk / Peter Smith.
Description: Lanham : Rowman & Littlefield, [2018] | Series: Tempo : a Rowman & Littlefield music series on rock, pop, and culture | Includes bibliographical references and index.
Identifiers: LCCN 2018026466 (print) | LCCN 2018027734 (ebook) | ISBN 9781442255593 (electronic) | ISBN 9781442255586 (cloth : alk. paper)
Subjects: LCSH: Sex Pistols (Musical group) | Punk rock music—History and criticism.
Classification: LCC ML421.S47 (ebook) | LCC ML421.S47 S65 2018 (print) | DDC 782.42166092/2—dc23
LC record available at https://lccn.loc.gov/2018026466

♾️™ The paper used in this publication meets the minimum requirements of American National Standard for Information Sciences Permanence of Paper for Printed Library Materials, ANSI/NISO Z39.48-1992.

Printed in the United States of America

CONTENTS

ACKNOWLEDGMENTS

Many thanks to the following who kindly allowed me to use their material within this book: Bill Gillum for his narrative account of the Pistols' gig at Middlesbrough Rock Garden; Peter Don't Care for his narrative account of the Pistols' gig at Wolverhampton Lafayette Club; and Tom Graves for allowing me to use "When the Sex Pistols Came to Memphis," which is his chapter in *Louise Brooks, Frank Zappa, & Other Charmers & Dreamers* by Tom Graves. Tom's chapter also appears on the www.guerrillamonsterfilms.com site of Mike McCarthy. Many thanks also to my wife, Marie Smith, and my son, David Smith, who spent many hours supporting me in the production of this text.

SERIES EDITOR'S FOREWORD

After barely holding together for three tumultuous years, the Sex Pistols were no more. Their influence on rock history, however, is disproportionately great for their years of being an active part of it, and that, in and of itself, was, perhaps, punk's secret weapon. Small footprint; big impact, all things considered, with plenty of crass, crude, and foul attitude to leave nothing tidy or settled once punk showed up. For author Peter Smith, he found in the Sex Pistols the makings of "a revolution of my own" from 1975 to 1978, and his contribution to the Tempo series marks the rise and fall of the Sex Pistols amid the cultural upheaval of the times, all of which he bore witness to in real time and which he shares here, writing as a music historian, cultural critic, and autobiographer.

For many fans, their first Sex Pistols concert was one of those "nights that changed my life" experiences, and Smith is no exception to having felt that way. Smith takes the good, bad, and tragic into account as the Sex Pistols rode, shaped, and defied the cultural currents that flowed from rock to pop to disco and punk. He ends his story as a survivor who appreciates the great irony of how even the Sex Pistols—once a great threat to Western civilization—have been accepted with pride into mainstream culture's archive of rebels.

Scott Calhoun
Series Editor

TIMELINE

World Events and Cultural Items

January 27, 1956: Elvis Presley releases "Heartbreak Hotel," signaling the start of rock 'n' roll.

November 22, 1963: John F. Kennedy is assassinated in Dallas, Texas.

January 19, 1971: Charles Manson and his "Family" are on trial for the murder of Sharon Tate. The Beatles' "Helter Skelter" is played at the trial because Manson believed the lyrics contain messages predicting the murders.

January 9, 1972: In the United Kingdom, miners go on strike for the first time since 1926.

February 9, 1972: British conservative government under Prime Minister Edward Heath declares a state of emergency. The British government announces three-day work week, introduced to save electricity.

Last US ground troops withdrawn from Vietnam.

Sex Pistols' Career

January 22, 1946: Malcolm McLaren is born.

September 3, 1955: Steve Jones is born.

January 31, 1956: John Lydon (Johnny Rotten) is born.

July 20, 1956: Paul Cook is born.

August 27, 1956: Glen Matlock is born.

May 10, 1957: John Simon Ritchie (Sid Vicious) is born.

October 1971: Malcolm McLaren opens the shop "Let It Rock" on 430 Kings Road, London, with girlfriend Vivienne Westwood.

1972: Steve Jones and Paul Cook form a band, known as "The Strand" or "The Swankers," with their friend Wally Nightingale.

UK unemployment rises to one million for the first time since the depression years of the 1930s.

June 16, 1972: David Bowie releases the LP *Ziggy Stardust and the Spiders from Mars*, which is a big influence on the Pistols and punk rock. Steve Jones attended the final Ziggy concert at Hammersmith Odeon, stealing some of the equipment.

November 7, 1972: President Richard Nixon was re-elected in one of the biggest landslides ever in US political history.

March 4, 1974: Conservative prime minister Edward Heath is succeeded by Labour prime minister Harold Wilson

1974: Glen Matlock joins as bass player. Matlock is working in Malcolm McLaren's King's Road shop Let It Rock.

April 6, 1974: ABBA win the Eurovision Song contest at Brighton, UK.

August 1974: The Nixon administration is engulfed in the Watergate scandal, which leads to the resignation of President Richard Nixon.

1974: Let It Rock is renamed "SEX."

February 11, 1975: Margaret Thatcher defeats Edward Heath and becomes the first female leader of the Conservative Party in the United Kingdom.

January 1975: Malcolm McLaren becomes manager of the New York Dolls.

April 30, 1975: The Vietnam War ends with the fall of Saigon.

1975: Malcolm McLaren returns from the United States after managing the New York Dolls and becomes manager of The Swankers. Wally Nightingale leaves and the band is renamed the Sex Pistols.

October 30, 1975: Peter Sutcliffe, the Yorkshire Ripper, commits his first murder.

1975: John Lydon auditions as singer in the King's Road shop, singing Alice Cooper's "18" in front of a jukebox.

August 15, 1975: The Birmingham Six are convicted of the Birmingham pub bombings, which were committed by the IRA. They are eventually released in 1991.

November 6, 1975: Sex Pistols play their first gig at Saint Martin's School of Art, London.

January 29, 1976: Twelve provisional IRA bombs explode in the West End of London.

Early 1976: Sex Pistols play in London and surrounding areas and begin to play their first gigs in the North of England.

March 16, 1976: Harold Wilson resigns as Prime Minister of the United Kingdom.

March 30, 1976: Sex Pistols play their first gig of many at 100 Club, London.

April 5, 1976: James Callaghan becomes Prime Minister of the United Kingdom.

Summer 1976: A long, hot summer in the United Kingdom, leading to a drought and the use of standpipes to provide water.

July 29, 1976: Son of Sam begins a series of murders, which terrorizes the city of New York for the coming year.

August 16, 1976: The Ramones make their first appearance at CBGBs nightclub in New York City.

August 21, 1976: The Rolling Stones perform to 120,000 people, including the author, at Knebworth Park, Hertfordshire, United Kingdom.

September 18, 1976: Queen perform a free concert in Hyde Park, London, to 150,000 people, including the author.

October 22, 1976: The Damned release "New Rose," the first UK punk rock single.

November 1976: Jimmy Carter wins the US presidential election.

December 15, 1976: UK chancellor Denis Healey negotiates a £2.3 billion loan from the International Monetary Fund.

1977 is a year of strikes and discontent in the United Kingdom and inflation is running at 15 percent.
January 17, 1977: Gary Gilmore is executed in the first execution since the reintroduction of the death penalty in the United States. He is the inspiration for the punk record "Gary Gilmore's Eyes" by UK band the Adverts.
January 20, 1977: Jimmy Carter succeeds Gerald Ford as the thirty-ninth president of the United States.

February 4, 1977: Fleetwood Mac release *Rumours*, their Grammy Award–winning mega successful album.

March 1, 1977: UK prime minister James Callaghan threatens to withdraw state assistance to auto manufacturer British

August 31, 1976: Sex Pistols play first punk rock festival at 100 Club, London.

September 11, 1976: The author sees Sex Pistols for the first time in Whitby, Yorkshire, and everything changes!

October 8, 1976: Sex Pistols sign with EMI for £40,000.

November 26, 1976: First single, "Anarchy in the U.K." is released on EMI.

December 1, 1976: Sex Pistols appear on the *Today* show with interviewer Bill Grundy. The band swear on daytime TV, causing national outrage.

December 3, 1976: "Anarchy in the UK" tour starts. The majority of dates are canceled because of the furor caused by the Bill Grundy incident.

January 1977: EMI sacks Sex Pistols.

February 28, 1977: Glen Matlock is fired from the band and replaced by Sid Vicious.

March 10, 1977: Sex Pistols sign to A&M Records.

Leyland unless it puts an end to strikes. The managers of British Leyland later threaten to dismiss forty thousand toolmakers in Birmingham.

March 16, 1977: Sex Pistols sacked by A&M Records.

April 8, 1977: The Clash release their debut album, *The Clash*, in the United Kingdom.

March 28, 1977: Sid Vicious debuts with Sex Pistols at Notre Dame Hall, London.

April 23, 1977: National Front marchers clash with anti-Nazi protesters in London.

April 30, 1977: Led Zeppelin set a world record attendance at the Pontiac Silverdome when 76,229 rock fans attend a concert on the group's 1977 North American tour.

May 17, 1977: Queen Elizabeth commences her Silver Jubilee tour in Glasgow, Scotland.

May 1977: Sex Pistols sign to Virgin Records.

May 25, 1977: The legendary film *Star Wars* opens in cinemas and becomes the highest-grossing film of its time.

May 27, 1977: "God Save the Queen" released on Virgin Records.

June 6–9, 1977: Silver Jubilee celebrations are held across the United Kingdom to celebrate Queen Elizabeth's twenty-five years on the throne.

June 7, 1977: Sex Pistols play on a riverboat sailing down the Thames as part of their own Silver Jubilee celebrations. The riverboat party is halted by the police.

June 20, 1977: Seventeen people are arrested during violent clashes between the police and pickets at the Grunwick film processing laboratory in the United Kingdom.

June 26, 1977: A sixteen-year-old shop assistant, Jayne Macdonald, is found stabbed to death in Leeds, United Kingdom, the fifth victim of the Yorkshire Ripper.

June 26, 1977: Elvis Presley performs his final concert at Market Square Arena, Indianapolis.

June 1977: Members of the band are attacked in the streets of London.

July 13, 1977: The New York City blackout lasts for twenty-five hours, resulting in looting and disorder.

July 1, 1977: "Pretty Vacant" is released as the band's third single.

August 16, 1977: Elvis Presley dies in his home, Graceland, at the age of forty-two. Seventy-five thousand fans line the streets of Memphis for his funeral on August 18.

August 19, 1977: SPOTS (Sex Pistols On Tour Secretly) tour opens in Wolverhampton.

August 25, 1977: Author attends Sex Pistols gig at Scarborough Penthouse club, Yorkshire.

October 3, 1977: Undertakers go on strike in London, leaving more than eight hundred corpses unburied.

October 14, 1977: "Holidays in the Sun" released as the band's fourth single.

November 10, 1977: The album *Saturday Night Fever*, the soundtrack of the same titled film and featuring the Bee Gees, is released. It becomes the best-selling album of all time, for that period.

October 28, 1977: *Never Mind the Bollocks* released. The album reaches number 1 in the UK album chart.

November 14, 1977: UK firefighters go on their first national strike, arguing for a 30-percent wage increase.

December 1977: Sex Pistols play "Never Mind the Bans" tour of the United Kingdom.

December 21, 1977: Four children die at a house fire in the United Kingdom as temporary fire engines run by the army, the Green Goddess, are sent to deal with the blaze while firefighters strike. One hundred nineteen people have now died because of fires since the strike started.

December 25, 1977: Sex Pistols play their final UK concerts at Huddersfield Ivanhoe's Club, Yorkshire. The concerts include an afternoon show for the children of striking firefighters and an evening concert for the public.

January 16, 1978: The firefighters' strike ends when fire crews accept an offer of a 10-percent pay raise and reduced working hours.

January 1978: Sex Pistols embark upon a tour of the United States.

January 25–27, 1978: The Great Blizzard of 1978 strikes the Ohio Valley and Great Lakes, killing seventy in the United States.

February 5–7, 1978: The northeastern US blizzard of 1978 hits New England and New York, killing one hundred and causing more than $520 million in damage.

January 14, 1978: Sex Pistols play their final gig at the Winterland Ballroom, San Francisco. Johnny Rotten ends the show with the famous words "ever felt cheated?"

February 16, 1978: In the United States, the Hillside Strangler, a serial killer in Los Angeles, claims a tenth and final victim.

June 12, 1978: In the United States, serial killer David Berkowitz, the "Son of Sam," is sentenced to 365 years in prison.

October 12, 1978: Nancy Spungen is found dead and Sid Vicious is charged with her murder.

May 4, 1979: The Conservative Party wins the UK general election and Margaret Thatcher becomes the country's first female prime minister, ending the rule of James Callaghan's Labour Party. Her rule is to lead to further social discontent.

February 1, 1979: Sid Vicious found dead by his mother. He had suffered a drug overdose.

INTRODUCTION

The Sex Pistols had a massive impact on popular music culture. They exploded onto the music scene in 1976, paving the way for a deluge of punk rock that would change the face of popular music forever. Punk is often characterized as three-chord thrash and being of limited musical merit; but these guys could really play. This book tracks the career of the Sex Pistols, from their early beginnings in late 1975, through to their all-too-soon, but perhaps inevitable, implosion in early 1978. The importance of the band, their impact on music and popular culture, and their seminal debut album are all discussed and reviewed alongside the cultural, political, and social events taking place in the world at the time.

In the early 1970s, I was a massive fan of Yes, Genesis, Led Zeppelin, Deep Purple, the Who, and the Rolling Stones. I loved those bands and went to see them in concert at every opportunity. My musical tastes also extended to pop; I recall attending great gigs where T Rex and Slade tore the place up. But things were beginning to change. I watched the Stones move from playing to two thousand fans in small theaters to stadiums and festivals, and audiences of two hundred thousand. Within a short four-year period, Led Zeppelin had gone from performing in venues so small I could almost touch Robert Plant while he prowled around the tiny stage in the Locarno Ballroom in Sunderland to being one of seventeen thousand fans watching them play at the other end of the soulless aircraft hangar that was London's Earls Court. Yes and Genesis had moved from playing short, intricate, and beautiful pop/rock to extended, convoluted prog-rock epics such as *Tales from Topographic Oceans* and *The Lamb Lies Down on Broadway*. The bands I had grown up with and followed so devotedly were beginning to turn their backs on their musical roots. They were losing the very soul of their music in a sea of pomposity, effects, and technology. Like many others, I was ready for something new; something more immediate and accessible. I'd missed out on being part of the musical and cultural revolutions of the 1960s; I was just that bit too young. I needed a revolution of my own; I had tried to find it in rock, but it was rapidly moving away from me.

The 1970s were a decade of dramatic change. A world oil crisis afflicted nations and unemployment had struck the Western world on a scale little known for decades. Environmental issues rose high on the agenda, and the public started to lose confidence in governments, realizing the potential hazards from the use of nuclear power and fearing the effects of pollution. In the United States, faith in the government ran especially low, owing to the Watergate scandal, which exposed the corruption of the presidency. While the Vietnam War had ended, and the threat of nuclear war was slowly receding because of détente, the United Kingdom labored under strikes, industrial actions, the "three-day week," inflation, power cuts, conflict in Northern Ireland and bombings in London, and the growth of the far-right movement. The hippies of the 1960s were growing up and becoming disillusioned as their visions of peace and love failed to become reality.

Young people were looking for something different and were taking their cues from music. In the United States, the New York Dolls, followed by the Ramones, Talking Heads, and Blondie, were spearheading the "new wave" movement in rock 'n' roll; on the other side of the Atlantic, the Sex Pistols, The Clash, and The Damned had gained their own followings. The revolution then in the air was one of raw sonic power. The Sex Pistols came to typify the edge of the punk spectrum, following in the wake of their sudden fame (and notoriety) with the release of their seminal debut album, *Never Mind the Bollocks*. While it is true the Sex Pistols flared briefly, that flaring was not only bright but also, for the music world, earth-shaking. It is a tale that unfolds against a backdrop of life in 1970s Britain, the Queen's Jubilee, and the political and cultural events of the time.

The Sex Pistols formed in London in 1975 and are often credited as being responsible for the UK punk rock movement. Although the origin and growth of UK punk is much more complex, the Sex Pistols unquestionably influenced and inspired many musicians to start their own bands. In their short, and incendiary, two-and-a-half-year career, they produced one of the most important and influential rock albums of all time, *Never Mind the Bollocks, Here's the Sex Pistols*, and released four of the most exciting, vital, and passionate singles of the 1970s (or, indeed, any other era). The original lineup of the Sex Pistols was singer Johnny Rotten (John Lydon), guitarist Steve Jones, bass player Glen Matlock, and drummer Paul Cook. Glen Matlock was replaced by Rotten's friend Sid Vicious in 1977. The Pistols were managed by artist and designer Malcolm McLaren, who with his partner, Vivienne Westwood, owned a shop in London's trendy King's Road.

Living in the North East of the United Kingdom, I was geographically and culturally removed from the massive changes in youth culture which were taking place in the south. London seemed so far away. I'd read of punk rock in *Sounds* and *New Musical Express*, the weekly music papers that I bought and devoured, and when I saw a tiny listing in *Sounds* for a Sex Pistols concert in Whitby, my girlfriend and I decided to go.

The concert took place in the White Horse Inn, a public house on a cliff overlooking Whitby town, which held a regular Saturday disco. Entrance was 50 pence, and the venue was far from full. The audience consisted of young locals dressed in their best disco gear. Their regular Saturday night routine was a few drinks, dancing to a live band and chart hits, topped by chips from a seafront fish shop on the way home. But this Saturday promised a very different experience, unlike anything they had seen before. The Sex Pistols walked from the corner of the room onto the stage, sneering at the crowd. They opened with "Anarchy in the U.K.": "a call to arms to the kids who believe that rock and roll was taken away from them" (Kent 1976b). Johnny Rotten was hanging off the mike stand, staring at the punters crowded on the dance floor. As they were playing their fifth song, the DJ sensed things weren't going well, that the venue had booked something they couldn't understand or handle. Before the Pistols could start the next song, he switched off the sound: "Thank you for tonight's band the Sex Pistols, now it's back to the disco." He returned to playing chart hits.

The music and the performance were deafening, shocking, exhilarating, and stunning. In that moment, everything changed for me. I was excited, intrigued, shocked, and excited. Rotten fascinated, scared, and motivated me at the same time. Others were similarly affected by their first experience of seeing the Pistols. Morrissey (2013) felt Rotten was a "striking Dickensian original," Peter Hook (2012) of Joy Division described his first Pistols experience as "a night that turned out to be the most important of my life."

A month later, the Sex Pistols appeared on the Bill Grundy television show, shocked everyone by swearing, and "altered the course of British popular music" (Hornby, 2007). The power and impact of the Pistols was clear. How much the impact was a result of design and how much chance is open to debate. McLaren (2007) saw the band as "my Sex Pistols: sexy, young, subversive and stylish boys" and argued that he was using them to "help me plot the downfall of this tired and fake culture." Morrissey (2013) saw "their riches" as "overwhelming" and felt that they were "not the saviours of culture, but the destruction of it." Licht (2005) argues that the Pistols were "manufactured by McLaren as a kind of art project."

This book follows and analyzes the short and explosive career of the Sex Pistols.

Chapter 1 covers the birth of the Sex Pistols. The music and ethic of the Sex Pistols did not appear sui generis. The band had been influenced by US new wave music, particularly that of the New York Dolls and Iggy Pop. But their roots also lay in 1960s beat, pop, and mod, drawing in particular on the path cut by the Small Faces and The Who. Malcolm McLaren, his partner Vivienne Westwood, and their King's Road shop SEX mixed a vision and attitude that helped formulate the Sex Pistols' ethos. Britain was ready for something new. Widespread dissatisfaction with the political and social situation was rampant, class divisions were deepening, unemployment was rising, and young people were feeling cheated. The Sex Pistols managed to capture the mood of those young and desperate souls, creating a mirror in which they could observe their own frustrations in action—and in art. Punk provided an outlet, cause, and direction that easily drew in working-class British youth. In punk, young people saw and felt an authenticity, vibrancy, immediacy, and ethos that excited, liberated, and empowered. By the summer of 1976, the Sex Pistols started to make their initial moves into the provinces and further afield to play gigs, including their legendary shows at Manchester Free Trade Hall—performances that catalysed the Manchester punk scene and resulted in the formation of Joy Division, The Fall, Buzzcocks, and The Smiths. In July, two new punk bands, The Clash and The Damned, appeared as support acts for the Sex Pistols. Things were starting to happen, and the scene was starting to make waves across the United Kingdom.

Chapter 2 covers the period from summer to autumn of 1976. That summer was one of the hottest on record in the United Kingdom, with a heat wave that lasted weeks. Musically, the old guard continued as if nothing were happening. The Rolling Stones played to two hundred thousand people in Knebworth Park on a hot August night, while Queen played a free concert in Hyde Park. Elton John and Kiki Dee hit number 1 in the United Kingdom singles charts for six weeks. Meanwhile, in the Irish Republic, a state of emergency had been declared prior to the introduction of antiterrorist legislation. British industry was in the grip of strong unions and was still recovering from the effects of inflation and recession. Drawing on this backdrop, in August 1976 the Sex Pistols began to record demos, drawing from their growing song catalog. A new song, "Anarchy in the U.K." premiered at their second gig in Manchester in July 1976. In September, the London 100 Club Punk Special showcased the new movement, featuring the Sex Pistols as headliners with support from seven other punk rock bands, including The Clash, Siouxsie and the Banshees, Buzzcocks, and The Damned. In October, the Sex Pistols caught the attention of and signed to major record label EMI, and on November 26, 1976, "Anarchy in the U.K." was released as a single. Described by Malcolm McLaren as "a call to arms to the kids who believe that rock and roll was taken away from them" (McLaren in Kent 1976), "Anarchy in the U.K." stormed the British airways. The crashing music and provocative lyrics—given the political, social, and cultural tensions of the time—turned the Sex Pistols into herald and heretic. Often sung to open their shows, "Anarchy in the U.K." and the in-your-face fearless authenticity of Johnny Rotten and the Sex Pistols outraged the public and excited fans.

On December 1, 1976, the Sex Pistols appeared on the Bill Grundy show, called Grundy "a f°°king rotter," and used the word "s°°t" on early evening television. With this event, the United Kingdom really became aware of punk rock. Within literal minutes, this incident de-

livered everything the youth of the United Kingdom had been waiting
for: a public display of arrogance, attitude, and freedom, alongside a
complete lack of fear.

Chapter 3 discusses the Bill Grundy incident, the far-ranging nature
of its impact, and the reverberations of shock and fear that it started.
The word "f**k" had been uttered on British television on only two
previous occasions. Glen Matlock was the first working-class guy to do
so on an early evening magazine program when, referring to the Sex
Pistols' record company advance, he said, "We f**king spent it." The
term appeared twice more from the mouth of Steve Jones over the next
few minutes, and viewers knew the Sex Pistols really *meant it*. To the
public and the mainstream media, their fears and prejudices were confirmed: these rockers were out to corrupt the youth, and they had to be
stopped. Before the Grundy incident, the Sex Pistols and punk were
barely a blip on the national screen; the next day, punk was a national
phenomenon. The front page of the *Daily Mirror* referred to the incident as "The Filth and the Fury"—a phrase that later appeared on T-
shirts and as the title of a movie about the Pistols. The Sex Pistols and
punk rock were demonized, and councils all over the United Kingdom
sought to ban this new music "cult." The incident destroyed the career
of Bill Grundy.

Chapter 4 tracks the Pistols' "Anarchy" tour, which kicked off on
December 6, 1976, at Leeds Polytechnic, having been cut from nineteen dates to three as a direct result of the commotion and outrage
caused by the Grundy debacle. The tour had originally been intended
to showcase the Sex Pistols, with support from The Clash, The Damned
(who were thrown off the tour after a few days), and, from the United
States, ex–New York Doll Johnny Thunders and his new band, The
Heartbreakers. Instead, the bands found themselves traveling around
the United Kingdom on a tour bus looking for gigs to play. It was a cold
winter, and the economic climate remained poor. Inflation stood at 16
percent and the government had just negotiated a £2.3 billion loan from
the International Monetary Fund. In January 1977, EMI, under media
and political pressure to do something about the outrageous "trash"
they had signed, released the Sex Pistols from their contract. Shortly
afterward, in February, Glen Matlock left and was replaced by Sid
Vicious, who was then still learning to play bass guitar. In March, the
Sex Pistols signed with A&M Records, but this did not last long when

the band, drunk at the time, behaved badly in the record label's offices and threatened a senior member of staff. Richard Branson's label, Virgin, then signed the band—their third record label in just over one year. With Virgin began the Sex Pistols' relations with the established music business.

Chapter 5 explores the Sex Pistols' exploits during June 1977. The Sex Pistols' second, and most controversial, single, "God Save the Queen," was released at the end of May to coincide with the celebrations for Queen Elizabeth II's Silver Jubilee. The record featured a sleeve, designed by Jamie Reid and named the greatest record cover of all time by *Q Magazine*, depicting the queen's eyes obscured by the song's title and "Sex Pistols" in the band's trademark cutout letters covering her mouth. Despite its banning, the song reached number 2 on the UK singles chart, with it reportedly being blocked from the number 1 spot for political reasons. The British monarchy remained popular with a large part of the population, and many viewed the jubilee as a moment of civic pride and a brief respite from the challenges facing the country. Because the Royal Family represented a unifying force that stood above the politics of the time, many took umbrage at the Sex Pistols' defiance. But a good number of British youth saw the jubilee as evidence of their disenfranchisement, and the queen as a symbol of everything wrong with their country. McLaren and the Sex Pistols had their own celebratory plans. On 7 June, during the week of royal events, they assembled with a group of friends, fans, and music journalists to take a boat trip down the Thames—a launch party for "God Save the Queen" that featured a short concert by the band. Hungry to play, the band delivered an incendiary performance for the small audience, singing "Anarchy in the U.K." as the boat passed the houses of Parliament. The party was raided and ultimately halted by the police, and a number of people were arrested.

Chapter 6 examines the growth of punk rock during the latter part of the summer of 1977. More and more young people aligned themselves with the new movement, some as a direct result of the success of "God Save the Queen." But they remained a minority, and violent attacks on punks were not uncommon. Johnny Rotten was attacked on a London street, and Pistols' drummer Paul Cook was also beaten. A Teddy Boy band even recorded a song called "The Punk Bashing Boogie." But violence wasn't limited to attacks on punks. In Lewisham, more than one hundred people were injured in violent street battles between left-wing demonstrators and the National Front. Over the August bank holiday weekend, more than fifty arrests were made as a result of street battles during the Notting Hill carnival. On soccer fields across the country and farther afield, organized hooliganism was ruining the experience for many. For most music fans, bland rock remained popular. Best-selling albums in the United Kingdom included ABBA's *Arrival*, Fleetwood Mac's *Rumours*, and the Eagles' *Hotel California*. In the United States, Robert Stigwood and the Bee Gees had *Saturday Night Fever* and disco music predominated. In the United Kingdom, punk bands were forming across the country and The Clash, The Damned, The Stranglers, and The Vibrators all released debut albums. Banned from playing and unable to tour openly, in the summer of 1977 the Pistols decided to play a series of secret club dates, or "guerrilla gigs." The "SPOTS" Tour (Sex Pistols On Tour Secretly) took place over the last week of August and the first week of September 1977. Sometimes termed the "Summer of Hate," in direct contrast to 1967's "Summer of Love," punk reflected the violent mood of what was a grim time in the United States, where several young girls died at the hands of Los Angeles' "Hillside Strangler" and the "Son of Sam" was stalking and killing young women in New York.

The Sex Pistols' debut album *Never Mind the Bollocks, Here's the Sex Pistols* was released on October 27, 1977. Its release was preceded by the singles "Pretty Vacant," which described perfectly the teenage apathy of the time, and "Holidays in the Sun," the lyrics of which were based on the Pistols' trip to Berlin and commented on the recent growth in low-cost package holidays. *Never Mind the Bollocks* proved one of the most important rock albums of all time.

Chapter 7 discusses the album, analyzing each of the songs in detail. The month of its release was not without national and international drama. Strikes in England had extended to London undertakers, which left eight hundred corpses unburied; political chaos ensued when former liberal leader Jeremy Thorpe denied allegations of attempted murder; and the Yorkshire Ripper had struck again. The imagery and iconography of the garish album cover and its shocking title should not have shocked, but it did—and the manager of a Nottingham record store went to trial on obscenity charges for displaying the album in his shop window.

The winter of 1977–1978 was cold and bleak. Union action continued in response to the imposition of a 5-percent maximum pay increase for public service workers at a time when inflation was running at 15 percent. When the thirty thousand–strong firefighters union failed to see its demand for a 30-percent pay increase met, the resulting strike saw the army called in to provide emergency cover. In the private sector, the UK auto industry had experienced a disastrous year, with foreign cars outselling British-built ones for the first time. It was truly a "Winter of Discontent" with widespread strikes, a vote of no confidence in the Labour Party, and ultimately a general election won by the Conservative Party that brought Margaret Thatcher into power. The Sex Pistols remained hungry to perform, particularly as new recruit Sid started to play bass much better. The band embarked on another short "Never Mind the Bans" series of guerrilla gigs across the United Kingdom in December 1977. At short notice, just as the tour started, a full-page advertisement appeared in the *New Musical Express* that showed crosses on a map but no locations or dates. It was to be the Sex Pistols final tour of the United Kingdom, playing their last gig in their home country at Huddersfield Ivanhoe's Club on Christmas Day 1977. They played two shows that day: an afternoon show for kids of striking firefighters, and an evening show for the public.

Chapter 8 tracks the final UK tour, discussing its political and social importance and how the Christmas Day concerts exposed another side of the punk band.

Chapter 9 covers the Sex Pistols' seven-date US tour, which took place in January 1978 and included dates mainly in the Deep South. The planning of the tour was surreal from the outset. Rather than book concerts in major "rock" cities like New York and Los Angeles, McLaren decided to target the Deep South. He booked the Sex Pistols for shows in Atlanta, Memphis, San Antonio, Baton Rouge, Dallas, and Tulsa. The tour was to end in San Francisco, which was the only major city where the audience was likely to welcome the British punk band. The dates were set up to ensure maximum culture clash, confrontation, and media interest. As a result, the audience consisted of people who were there out of curiosity and a large contingent who attended just to cause trouble. The band members were not in good shape at the time, and the tour was plagued by infighting and hostile audience reactions. Sid Vicious began to fully live up to his image as the out-of-control rock star, Johnny Rotten became quite ill, and Jones and Cook felt isolated from the other two members of the band. Sid suffered from heroin addiction, overdosed, and was admitted to the hospital. The Sex Pistols played their final concert at San Francisco's Winterland Ballroom on January 14, 1978. The gig ended with Rotten uttering the now famous line, "Ever get the feeling you've been cheated?" On January 17, the Sex Pistols split up.

After their break-up, Johnny Rotten reverted to his real name, John Lydon, and formed Public Image Limited, a post-punk band that played experimental music far removed from the classic punk rock of the Sex Pistols. Jones and Cook teamed up with escaped train robber Ronnie Biggs and recorded a new Pistols single. McLaren continued work on a Pistols movie, which was released as *The Great Rock 'n' Roll Swindle* in 1980. On October 12, 1978, Sid Vicious' girlfriend Nancy Spungen was found dead in their New York hotel room. Sid was charged with her murder, although he claimed to have no memory of what had occurred. Vicious died of an overdose on February 2, 1979. In 1996, the Sex Pistols original line-up of John Lydon, Glen Matlock, Steve Jones, and Paul Cook reformed for the "Filthy Lucre" world tour, which included seventy concerts for more people than the Sex Pistols ever played to originally. This was followed by further reunions in 2002 and 2007. An epilogue to the book covers the Pistols later activities and the reunions and reflects on their legacy and how it has shaped modern music and culture.

The Sex Pistols helped shape modern music, fashion, and culture. Without the Pistols, there would be no Nirvana, no Green Day, or countless other bands. In 2006, Vivienne Westwood became a Dame. Malcolm McLaren died in 2010; his coffin was sprayed "Too Fast To Live; Too Young To Die." In 2008, John Lydon appeared in a television advertising campaign for Country Life butter wearing a tweed suit— every inch the country gent.

I

THE BIRTH OF THE SEX PISTOLS

Before Summer 1976

The 1970s was a decade of great change. In some ways, and particularly in economic terms, it was possibly the worst decade since the Great Depression of the 1930s. This was a decade of political turmoil, high inflation, rising unemployment, and industrial unrest. People were starting to view the hippie movement of the 1960s as too idealistic, yet the progressive values on which it was based, such as increasing political awareness and political and economic liberty of women, remained as strong and relevant as ever. Tom Wolfe (1976) called the 1970s the "'Me' decade" referring to a general new attitude of Americans toward individualism.

In Britain the economy had been strong with low unemployment throughout the 1960s. Toward the start of the new decade, however, unemployment started to rise, and a conservative government came into power in 1970. Britain suffered severe inflation, strikes, and union power, which neither the conservative government nor the new Labour Party, which succeeded it in 1974, was able to halt. By 1972, unemployment in Britain had exceeded one million. This, along with the impact of an international oil crisis, led to the imposition of a three-day work week for many in 1973–1974. This extreme industrial strife, along with rising inflation and unemployment, led Britain to being nicknamed the "sick man of Europe." It was against this backdrop, and in part as a result of it, that one of the most significant changes in modern popular music was about to take place.

The UK music scene of the 1970s was in a state of change, yet at the same time, it was also stagnating. Music had moved a long way from the pop and rock scene that had been born in, and was very much a part of, the 1960s. Bands were experimenting with new instruments and more complex concepts. Music fans in the 1960s were lucky enough to be able to see their heroes in small venues, such as ballrooms and clubs with capacities of less than two thousand. I remember standing in line for twenty-eight hours to buy tickets for the Rolling Stones at Newcastle City Hall, being crushed a few feet away from Led Zeppelin in a dangerously crammed Locarno Ballroom in Sunderland, watching David Bowie, as Ziggy Stardust, play to a half-full Newcastle City Hall, and cheering as Pete Townshend smashed his guitar into pieces in the Newcastle Odeon. There was a great intimacy to gigs like that. You could almost touch the band; the volume shook you; the power of the performance and the emotional rush of the crowd's reaction were *exhilarating*. You felt alive and refreshed and would talk about the experiences for days afterward (Smith 2015c).

But our heroes were starting to move away from us. The demand for rock concerts was growing, and bands needed to perform to larger crowds. Bands were starting to play in massive hangars and exhibition centers such as Wembley Empire Pool and Earls Court. These halls had never been designed for music performances. The sound was poor, visuals were low grade or nonexistent, and we watched tiny figures on a small stage that seemed miles away—as if we were watching the performance at a cinema, or on the television. Feelings of intimacy and personal connection were lost, and the performers were becoming distant—metaphorically and physically.

For their 1975 "tour" Led Zeppelin played five nights at Earls Court Arena, London (capacity seventeen thousand). The venue had been used for concerts before, notably one by David Bowie, at which the sound was reportedly atrocious: "one doubts whether more than half were able to even see what was going down on-stage, while the sound system veered from adequate to diabolical to totally inaudible" (Kent 1973). There was no support act and Zeppelin played a long set, approximately three hours each night. This was the first chance for UK fans to see the band in three years. Tickets went on sale to in-person applicants; I stood in line all night outside Virgin Records, New-castle, with a group of friends. We were all heavily into rock music and seeing Zeppelin was a big thing.

The Who were also out to prove themselves as "The Greatest Rock and Roll Band in the World" (there was little to choose between them, Zeppelin, and the Stones) and played legendary concerts at Charlton athletic field. The Who selected the field at Charlton ground because, according to Townshend, it had "particular acoustic qualities" and of-fered "excellent views of the stage from the terraces" (Neill and Kent 2007). The concert was intended to have an attendance limit of fifty-thousand fans, but breakdowns in security resulted in many additional people getting in, and an estimated crowd of eighty thousand was let in. There was a long wait before The Who took the stage, and several reports recall an atmosphere of violence. It was a very hot day and there were fights on the terraces, a heavy smell of dope with many people openly smoking joints, and lots of cans thrown around throughout the day.

It wasn't just the concert experience that was changing. Genesis, Yes, and Emerson Lake and Palmer were championing "prog-rock" (progressive rock), a brand of rock music with extended solos and classi-cal pretensions. Records were now being released as triple-album sets. Per Ian Anderson of Jethro Tull: "Prog Rock . . . has different connotations—of grandeur and pomposity. Back then, when we were doing *Thick as a Brick*, bands like Yes and Emerson Lake and Palmer were already gaining a reputation for being a little pompous and show-ing off with their music" (Deriso 2014). Your average kid in the east end of London, in Birmingham, Glasgow, or Sheffield, couldn't relate to this or afford the price of a triple album or a concert ticket. It was time for change.

The early 1970s music scene was also characterized by the emer-gence of glam rock in the form of David Bowie, T Rex, Roxy Music, and Mott the Hoople. Glam was both a reaction to and a natural develop-ment of psychedelia and was musically diverse, as much a fashion and style as a musical subgenre. Visually, glam was characterized with outra-geous clothes, makeup, hairstyles, and massive platform boots. American glam included the New York Dolls and Alice Cooper. Marc Bolan and David Bowie are good examples of the developments from 1960s beat and psychedelia into glam rock. Both stars had toyed with the mod and psychedelic scene and they both entered the 1970s as full-fledged glam rock stars, wearing makeup and proudly and outrageously displaying sexual and gender ambiguity. Bolan went electric, shortened his band's name from Tyrannosaurus Rex to T Rex, and rediscovered rock 'n' roll, borrowing riffs from Chuck Berry. Bowie revisited themes from science fiction, which had been successful for him in the 1960s in the form of the hit single "Space Oddity," and was reborn as Ziggy Stardust.

There was also a burgeoning pub rock scene in London, with bands like Dr Feelgood, the Count Bishops, Kilburn and the High Roads, and Ducks Deluxe, all of whom played a blend of R&B and rock 'n' roll. Pub rock enjoyed a back-to-basics attitude as a direct reaction against the excesses of progressive music and glam. The movement rejected concert hall and stadium venues and tried to return live music to the small pubs and clubs from whence it came. Pub rock was nasty, rocking, and sweaty. The bands would dress in denim or lumberjack shirts and scruffy jeans and looked deeply menacing and threatening. There was no image, no flash; band and audience were essentially the same. The music was basic rhythm and blues, stripped back to basics and reminiscent of the sounds of the early Rolling Stones and the Yardbirds.

Glam and pub rock were both strong influences on punk rock. Mick Houghton (1975) declares the term "punk" as being "bandied about an awful lot" and that it was being used to describe "almost any rock performer who camps it up to any degree, on or off-stage, or who displays an arrogance and contempt for his audience." Houghton relates the origin of the term "punk" to the historic album collection *Nuggets! Original Artefacts of the First Psychedelic Era, 1965–1968* released in 1972. He asks, "So what is punk rock?" referring to the definition of the word as an attitude meaning rotten or worthless, "totally ephemeral," and

> not to be taken seriously. . . . Vintage punk rock is less a style than a lack of style, defined by a crude simplicity—thin sounding Vox organs, 4/4 drumming, barely in time, and primer stage guitar playing, riffy fuzztones and later jangly chords, all fed through cheap Fender amps. The singer's stance was important, an aggressive swagger to counter his lousy adenoidal weak voice. . . . Punk rock songs dealt typically with teenage obsessions, frustrations and hang-ups over love and growing up. . . . Punk rock may have bordered on the realms of

bad musical taste but it *was* the genuine article. Street music, or rather garage music, which was never manufactured behind the scenes. Whatever else, the punk rock groups were people's groups— and that was important. (Houghton 1975)

Rock journalist Nick Kent returned from a visit to New York, having been there to check out the growing new wave scene in the form of bands like Television, the Ramones, and Patti Smith, and noted the lack of a similar scene in London, and the fact that

> just about every band with the marked exception of the unique and very wonderful Roogalator and also, possibly, The Sex Pistols (them- selves a rather obvious New York consciousness band who fortunate- ly anchor this pitch firmly within their Shepherd's Bush origins and outlook), seem totally unwilling to even dare commit themselves to commenting on their environment, to develop a decently relevant attitude to current times. (Kent 1976b)

MALCOLM MCLAREN, VIVIENNE WESTWOOD, AND THE KING'S ROAD

Malcolm McLaren and Vivienne Westwood are key figures in the story of the Sex Pistols. Malcolm McLaren was born on January 22, 1946. With art college training, his early philosophy was "To be bad is good . . . to be good is simply boring," which he claimed his grandmoth- er, who raised him, had taught him (in an interview by Andrew Denton on *Enough Rope*).

McLaren was attracted by the stance and philosophy of the Situa- tionists. The Situationists were an international organization of revolu- tionaries, including intellectuals and artists, that was formed in 1957 and existed until the early 1970s. They derived their philosophical stance from the work of Marx, and also drew from the works of Dada and from surrealism. Theirs was a social movement, inherently anti- establishment and anti-capitalist in its stance. They believed in creating provocative and anarchic situations that would challenge the establish- ment and liberate.

The Situationists took the theories of Marx and others and at- tempted to relate them to twentieth-century capitalism. They believed that many of Marx's original concepts, such as alienation and fixation with commodity, still applied and had relevance in the modern context. They argued that the successes of modern society, such as technological advances, increased income, and more leisure time, were far out-weighed by the disadvantages of alienation and social dysfunction. One of the core concepts of the Situationist manifesto was the spectacle, which referred to the increasing reliance and focus on commodities rather than individual expression.

In his essential Situationist text *The Society of the Spectacle*, Debord (1967) argues that: "All that once was directly lived has become mere representation" (Thesis 1). Debord goes on to observe "the decline of being into having and having into merely appearing" (Thesis 17) in the "historical moment at which the commodity completes its colonization of social life" (Thesis 44). The Situationists set out to confront and destroy the spectacle by constructing situations in which individuals could become liberated and again experience authenticity, life, desire, and adventure. The movement soon developed from its artistic roots into something much more political and revolutionary, and it was huge-ly influential in the May 1968 Paris riots. On May 13, 1968, French workers joined student protests in Paris as part of a one-day general strike, and eight hundred thousand people marched through the capital demanding change, as the climax of days of unrest and riots. Many of the protesters were opening carrying banners displaying Situationist slogans. McLaren attempted to join his friends at the events in Paris but failed to do so. He was, however, greatly influenced by the events and political ideologies of the Situationists, which he would apply a few years later in the context of punk and the Sex Pistols.

Vivienne Swire was born on April 8, 1941. She attended the Harrow School of Art but didn't enjoy the experience: "I didn't know how a working-class girl like me could possibly make a living in the art world." She became a school teacher. However, she continued to make her own jewelery, which she sold from a stall in the Portobello Market. In 1962, she married Derek Westwood. Vivienne Westwood met Malcolm McLaren in the late 1960s, which led to the end of her marriage. They moved in together in a council flat in Clapham. In 1971, they opened a boutique at 430 King's Road called Let It Rock.

In the 1960s, King's Road had become a focal point for youth culture with "an endless frieze of mini-skirted, booted, fair-haired angular angels" (Westwood 2018). Young mods would flock to the boutiques to buy the latest fashions and simply to be seen. It was to become a center for the counterculture and would house famous clothing shops, such as the exotically named Granny Takes a Trip. It was the ideal location for a shop that would begin to enact McLaren's vision. Let It Rock initially sold Teddy Boy clothes, drape jackets, and drainpipe trousers. McLaren and Westwood would, however, soon find the Teddy Boy scene limiting. In 1973, their vision expanded, and the shop was renamed Too Fast to Live Too Young to Die. It was during 1973 that McLaren visited New York, met the glam proto-punk band the New York Dolls, and started to design and supply their stage wear. The clothes that they were designing at that point used materials such as leather and latex and were heavily influenced by fetishism. In 1974, the shop was again renamed, this time with the provocative moniker SEX. In early 1975, McLaren and Westwood designed red patent leather stage costumes for the New York Dolls that included a Communist-style hammer-and-sickle motif. McLaren became the manager of the Dolls for a short period prior to their split in 1975. All of these influences—the 1960s, fashion, mod, glam, the Situationists, fetishism, the Dolls, and glam—were to come together in the concept that was soon to surface as the Sex Pistols.

THE BIRTH OF THE SEX PISTOLS

The roots of the Sex Pistols date back to 1972 when schoolmates Paul Cook, Steve Jones, and "Wally" Nightingale formed a band called The Strand, named after the Roxy Music song.

> Paul was in my class at school; Steve was in the lower class. . . . I started to try to get a group together. I had a guitar and an amplifier, a Les Paul copy. After I left school, I started to hang around with them, 'cos I liked Steve. He was funny, and things happened around him. He would make them happen. None of the others would have formed a group. Paul was heavily into an apprenticeship as an electrician. Steve was going to be a petty criminal, as simple as that. We made a hell of a racket and the woman who lived over the road was always banging on the door. (Cramp 2006)

The Strand acquired much of their gear by stealing equipment from gigs they attended, including David Bowie's final shows as Ziggy Stardust at Hammersmith Odeon in July 1973. "The security guard was asleep," recalled Wally in 1993. "Steve and I walked onstage with a pair of pliers and took the whole PA" (Nightingale 1993).

The three friends would hang around Let It Rock. In 1973, Glen Matlock, who worked in the shop, joined as bass player. By this time, the name of the shop had changed to Too Fast to Live Too Young to Die. The lineup of the band, which changed its name to the Swankers, was Steve Jones (vocals), Wally Nightingale (guitar), Glen Matlock (bass), and Paul Cook (drums). They began to rehearse regularly and soon Steve Jones started to play guitar. Wally's dad helped them find rehearsal rooms in a studio that belonged to the Hammersmith Council. The Swankers' set consisted of cover versions of songs by The Who and the Small Faces. By 1974, Malcolm's shop had changed its name to SEX and was selling rubber and leather sex fetish clothes. McLaren was showing an interest in managing the band, who became the "Sex Pistols," taking their name from the shop. In 1975, he became the band's full-time manager, and Wally was edged out. "We played Rod Stewart covers like 'It's All Over Now,' 'Twisting the Night Away,' and Small Faces stuff like 'All Or Nothing' or 'Sha-La-La-La-Lee.' We pumped it out, but Steve wasn't a good singer. He really wanted to be like Rod Stewart, but there was something holding him back. Steve was playing guitar behind my back. I was too naive to think he wanted my position in the group. Malcolm was there, and they just said, 'You're not in the group anymore.' It was very hard, I was so gutted that I didn't say anything" (Wally Nightingale). McLaren had just returned from the United States where he had been managing the New York Dolls. He wanted to try out his newly developed managerial skills on a home-grown act. Malcolm brought back a Les Paul guitar from New York that had belonged to the Dolls, which he gave to Steve.

Sometime in the summer of 1975 the paths of McLaren, the Sex Pistols, and a young John Lydon would cross. Steve Jones had noticed a guy who looked "a bit different" in McLaren's clothing shop, and Bernie Rhodes, one of McLaren's associates, saw the same guy on King's Road complete with short, spikey green hair and a homemade "I HATE Pink Floyd" T-shirt. This guy was John Lydon, and McLaren and the band felt he had exactly the sort of image and attitude that they were looking for. "Rotten looked really interesting, there was something about him that magnetized you to him. He had all this punk stuff on, the safety pins and everything. He was wild looking. His brothers were boot boys. So he came down and I really didn't like him at all, because of his attitude. He seemed like a real prick" (Jones 2018).

Lydon was somewhat reluctant to join but was persuaded to audition in the shop. His audition was apparently almost a joke with Lydon launching into "a series of self-mocking fits, hunches, and weird dances, while the others fell about laughing" (Sex Pistols online biography 2018).

> I'd go to King's Road just to annoy people. . . . What was there to do then? There was Soul boys and Roxy Music kind of clothes: all that was naff, very weedy and not going anywhere. People were very stiff and boring. I was bored with everything. . . . Malcolm asked me if I wanted to be in a band. I thought they must be joking. It seemed very cynical, and that really pissed off Steve. He was a bit thick, and he couldn't make out what I was talking about. . . . I couldn't sing a note. The only song I could cope with was Alice Cooper's "Eighteen." I just gyrated like a belly dancer. Malcolm thought, Yes, he's the one. Paul thought it was a joke and couldn't have cared less. Steve was really annoyed because he instantly hated me.
> (Lydon 2018)

The guys were sufficiently impressed by John's crazy, fearless attitude to offer him the job as their front man. They realized that there was no one else like him. The fact that he couldn't sing didn't matter; he had the image and look that they were searching for, and a stare that could burn right through you. Lydon was soon to be named Rotten, apparently because of his green and decaying teeth. The Sex Pistols started rehearsing seriously and began to write their own material with Rotten providing the lyrics and Matlock (and sometimes Jones) creating the music. Rotten provided new impetus and motivation and their set also included songs by Iggy and the Stooges, as well as mod classics by The Who and the Small Faces along with their own songs. An old Swankers song, "Scarface," became "Did You No Wrong" with Rotten rewriting the lyrics. New original songs "Seventeen" and "Submission" also emerged during this period. The band rehearsed in the Crunchy Frog, a studio in London's dockland.

On November 6, 1975, the Sex Pistols played their first gig supporting Bazooka Joe (featuring a young Adam Ant) at Saint Martin's School
of Art in London. There was a beautiful ramshackle amateurishness
about an early Pistols performance. Davies wrote of how "lack of musical skill itself removed barriers between performer and audience" (1996, 23); however, the same lack of musical skill created barriers with others. There was a sense of "Englishness" (Adams 2008,
469–88) about the Pistols, which you could hear in the lyrics, the cockney accents, and in the street urchin image of Rotten. Adams (2008)
describes punk as a bricolage of popular English culture, politics, and
history and argues that the Sex Pistols can only be understood within
the context of English history of that time. Garnett also argues that
punk was "of its time" and that it would soon pass because "the space
within which it operated was closed down" (1999, 17–30).

PUNK AND NEW WAVE

The term "new wave" music was first used to describe a new rock music
genre in the early 1970s by rock journalists Dave Marsh, who was writ-
ing for *Rolling Stone* magazine in the United States, and Nick Kent,
who was writing for the *New Musical Express* in the United Kingdom.
Dave Marsh, writing in *Melody Maker* in 1973, reported on the growing
New York scene, attributed its roots to Lou Reed and the Velvet
Underground, and mentioned a dozen or so new acts, including the
New York Dolls, "who epitomise the glitter scene," Teenage Lust,
formed by former members of hippie-activist band David Peel and the
East Side (famous for their albums *Have a Marijuana* and *The Pope
Smokes Dope*), and Queen Elisabeth, whose act featured "all manner of
sexual outrage" and Wayne County, who went on to front punk band
The Electric Chair and transgendered to Jayne County in 1979. The
focus for the new wave scene was Max's Kansas City, a "legendary dive
that served as a hangout for Andy Warhol's bunch, the late '60s rock
scene and more decadence than even its management cares to recall."
(Marsh 1972) Marsh (1973) also included heavy rock band Blue Oyster
Cult ("an older, more aloof group than the Dolls . . . the Cult members
do solos . . . their dress is grubby motorcycle punk") and glam metal
rockers Kiss in his coverage of the early scene.

The New York Dolls arrived and galvanized the entire scene. Real glam trash. Beautiful. They proved it was possible to be trashy and good at the same time. Kicked everyone into action at a desperate moment. They saved us all. At that moment, I was drawing lines into New York and the Velvets, European avant garde and electronic music, previous generation's Brit Psychedelia plus a ragged sort of insulting glam. I guess this was the start of the New Wave. By the way, whoever coined that New Wave byline is my hero. Because a New Wave is precisely what it was—and precisely what was needed at that moment. (Foxx, 2008)

In 1973, a new venue, CBGBs (Country, Blue Grass, and Blues), opened in the Bowery in New York City. CBGBs had been a biker bar and drinking hangout and was transformed into the new home for new wave bands like the Ramones, Television, the Patti Smith Group, Blondie, and the Talking Heads.

By 1976, all of the mainstream UK music papers, *Melody Maker*, *New Musical Express*, and *Sounds* were writing about the new punk movement. Wayne Robins (1976) wrote in *Newsday* listing the Talking Heads, the Ramones, the Heartbreakers, the Shirts, and Television as the better-known of the New York bands, often categorized under the catch-all "punk rock," that were attracting rock fans to clubs like CBGBs, Mothers, and Max's Kansas City. Robins recognized that the bands had a variety of musical styles and competence and that some, such as Television and the Talking Heads, were capable of "startling innovation," while others were "dreadfully derivative." One common feature of the bands was their dress. They all had short hair and chose to perform in their street clothes: T-shirts, jeans, and leather jackets. These guys were definitely post-glitter, and not in any way hippies.

The genre was so well developed by the summer of 1976 that Giovanni Dadomo (1976) felt it necessary to write "The A–Z of Punk" in *Sounds*. Dadomo felt that punk was as much a question of attitude, dress, and style as it was musical content. By the summer of 1976 punk had its own magazine in the form of fanzine *Sniffin' Glue* started by Mark Perry. The name of the magazine was derived from the Ramones song "Now I Wanna Sniff Some Glue." The first issue, which featured articles on the Ramones and Blue Oyster Cult, sold fifty copies, but circulation soon increased to fifteen thousand. "*Sniffin' Glue* was not so much badly written as barely written; grammar was non-existent, layout was haphazard, headlines were usually just written in felt tip, swear-words were often used in lieu of a reasoned argument . . . all of which gave *Sniffin' Glue* its urgency and relevance" (Fletcher 2001).

The terms "punk" and "new wave" were used somewhat inter-changeably, with "new wave" perhaps used more to describe the scene in the United States, and "punk" used more in the UK context. Music historian Vernon Joynson (2001) states that new wave emerged in the United Kingdom in late 1976, when many bands began disassociating themselves from punk: "For a while in 1976 and 1977 the terms punk and new wave were largely interchangeable. By 1978, things were be-ginning to change, although the dividing line between punk and new wave was never very clear." The Sex Pistols were very definitely *punk* and not *new wave*. Indeed, the Pistols were *the definitive* punk band. Theirs was the music of the London street, drawing from the US garage band sounds of the 1960s with heavy traces of UK mod and beat.

EARLY GIGS

Britain was ready for something new. Widespread dissatisfaction with the political and social situation was rampant. Britain was experiencing industrial strife on a scale it had not seen since the end of World War II: class divisions were deepening, unemployment was rising, and young people were feeling cheated. The Sex Pistols managed to capture the mood of those young and desperate souls, creating a mirror in which they could observe their own frustrations in action—and in art. The social and political context, McLaren's ideals, dissatisfaction with the direction of pop and rock music, lack of faith in a system that seemed to subsist on failing even as it lied to young people—all contributed to the Sex Pistols' phenomenal rise.

Mark Perry (founder of punk fanzine *Sniffin' Glue*):

> Early in 1976 I started reading in NME about a new "punk" scene which was developing in New York. Like London's pub rock scene, it revolved around small venues such as CBGBs and Max's Kansas City. The NME writers made it all sound new and exciting and I could sense that this was not an R&B scene, which us basically what the UK pub rock scene was all about. The band that really caught my imagination was The Ramones. . . . I bought the first Ramones album

on import and it completely blew me away. I'd never heard anything so exciting." (2009)

The Sex Pistols are a force, you get that feeling from their audience and it sticks in your mind. The clothes, the hair and even the attitude of the audience has a direct link to the band. . . . As the Pistols pounded out their music the image was in every corner of the club. Their sound is pure energy, you can't explain it in stupid words— you've got to experience it to understand. . . . Oh, Yeh, Rotten's this decade's FACE. (Perry 1976, 7)

On February 12, 1976, the Sex Pistols played at London's legendary Marquee Club as the opening act for Eddie & the Hot Rods. This was the band's first public concert in the capital, and it was fitting that it took place at the Marquee, which was one the most important London venues in the history of rock and pop. The Marquee had been an essential home and meeting point for artists and bands of the 1960s and had hosted gigs by the Rolling Stones, Cream, and Hendrix; so it was an ideal place for punk to be born. The Hot Rods were seen at the time as the Pistols' major competitors; however, their music was much more straightforward rock 'n' roll, and very different to the raw basic thrash of McLaren's boys. Neil Spencer, writing in the *New Musical Express*, warned us, "Don't look over your shoulder but the Sex Pistols are coming," and reported Steve Jones' prophetic comment "We're not into music, we're into chaos" (Spencer 1976). Valentine's Day saw the Sex Pistols playing at artist Andrew Logan's exclusive Valentine's Ball, which was attended by the young and trendy and was also reported in the *Sunday Times*.

During the following months, the Sex Pistols played concerts at key London venues. On March 30, 1976, they headlined for the first time at the prestigious 100 Club in central London, along Oxford Street. The 100 Club was to become an important venue in the development of punk and would host the first punk festival later in the year. On April 4, the Sex Pistols started a residency at the El Paradiso strip club and Rotten was interviewed by *Sounds* magazine: "I hate hippies and what they stand for. I hate long hair. I hate pub bands. . . . I want people to see us and start something, or else I'm just wasting my time" (Ingham 1976). On April 23, a Pistols appearance at the Nashville was marred by violence when a fight broke out in the crowd.

The Sex Pistols then started to make their initial moves into the provinces, at first playing gigs on the outskirts of London before venturing farther up into the North of England, including shows in Yorkshire. Their first visit to the North was in May 1976, when they played concerts in Northallerton, Scarborough, and Middlesbrough. Those gigs were attended by Pauline Murray, who would soon form the punk band Penetration: "Then we saw the Sex Pistols in Northallerton, in this tiny club. A short while later they played with the Doctors of Madness in Middlesbrough and they wiped them out. They wiped a lot of bands out. It sounds a cliché now but I saw it happen" (Savage 2015). The gigs were barely publicized; Murray found out about them through personal contact with McLaren. Many of the venues that the Pistols were playing were less than obvious, away from big cities. How much this was planned by McLaren, and whether he was a "Fagin for our times" (Jones, in Smith, 2015), sending his urchins out to gain some spoils is debatable. Much of the history of the time has been gathered through oral histories of the players and suffers from exaggeration and the problems of faded memory (Medhurst 1999, 219–31).

The Pistols also played legendary gigs at Manchester Lesser Free Trade Hall, which have been written about by many authors, including David Nolan (2006) in *I Swear I Was There: The Gig That Changed the World* and Sean Albiez (2005) in *Print the Truth, Not the Legend*. They are often referred to as a single gig, when there were in fact two concerts: one on June 4, 1976, and the other on July 20, 1976. The June gig has gained almost mythical status, with many people claiming that they were there. It is often quoted as the single event that created the birth of punk outside of London, led to the Manchester punk scene, and then to the famous Hacienda club, and in turn helped to create a dance and club culture that swept the world.

The Lesser Free Trade Hall held 150 to 200 people, and accounts of those who really did attend (Nolan 2006) suggest that the June gig was poorly attended with no more than fifty in the audience. The concert was organized by two Manchester students, Howard Devoto and Pete Shelley, who had traveled to London to find McLaren's shop and persuade him to bring the band to the North West. Devoto and Shelley would soon form their own punk band, the Buzzcocks. The support act at the June concert was a heavy rock band called Solstice; the Buzzcocks had planned to appear but hadn't rehearsed enough to be able to do so. A second concert, which attracted a capacity crowd, was held a few weeks later in the same venue. By the time of this gig, Howard Devoto and Pete Shelley had rehearsed their new band and felt confident enough for the Buzzcocks to play their first gig. Manchester punk band Slaughter and the Dogs also played. John Ingham (1976) describes the crowd as "David Bowie lookalikes," "Neanderthals in stringy hair and leather . . . pounding seats to oblivion" and "six rows of very straight looking people at the back who sat there very vacant all evening." He reports that the Pistols went down well with the Northern crowd, and were greeted with "a wild ovation." He also notes the rapid improvement that the Pistols were making from gig to gig, and that a new song, "Anarchy in the UK," was a highpoint of the concert. "For an encore, John tore up his shirt."

What is clear is that also in the audience at one of those two gigs were Morrissey, who went on to form The Smiths; Peter Hook and Bernard Sumner who soon formed Joy Division; Mark E. Smith who went on to lead The Fall; Paul Morley, who became a music journalist and writer; and Mick Hucknell, who formed Simply Red.

"That was it, that was the day, that was the time, that was the year, that was the precise moment when everything took a left turn" (Nolan 2006). Morley (2006), writing in *The Guardian* on June 4, 1976, lists the gig as one of the fifty key events in the history of indie music and describes the "yokel" audience as "scruffy, isolated avant garde music fans motivated to constantly search out new music." David Nolan depicts the audience as a group of long-haired male music fans, who really didn't know what to make of the young ramshackle Pistols. A month later things were different. The hall was full and an excited crowd were starting to understand the importance of punk and find their roles. The trousers were narrower, the hair shorter, and some people actually danced, although whether they pogoed is debatable.

Peter Hook (2012) recalls that at the gig, "there were no punks yet . . . a pretty standard rock band . . . what made them special . . . was Johnny Rotten" (37–38). Laing (Jones, in Smith 2015) refers to the shock aspects of the Sex Pistols performance as a "calculated assault on the conventional audience/performer relationship." "My life changed the moment that I saw the Sex Pistols," says Howard Devoto. "Suddenly there was a direction" (Savage 2005). The concept of the epiphany at gigs is well documented. For example, during his radio program, John

Peel would narrate the significant aspects of his life through "a series of watershed moments of epiphany" (Long 2006, 25).

Pistols' bassist Matlock discusses these excursions to the provinces in Savage (2005): "And this bloke, I'm not kidding, with a Tom Jones tux, gets up and goes 'All right ladies and gentlemen they've come all the way from London tonight, here for you in cabaret, the Sex Pistols.' Then we went off to another place and couldn't get there because the van wasn't powerful enough, and we had to get up this hill, and there was this long detour, miles around. There was seven of us in this Transit, and all the equipment and the PA." Savage (2005) reports a pattern in most early forays to the provinces: "rejection by most people and instant identification on the part of a tiny but significant minority."

There was something about the Sex Pistols that was all at once authentic, raw, innocent, dangerous, alarming: it was as if the band, and Rotten in particular, were driven by a chaotic and manic passion. Rotten donned the mask of Shakespeare's "absolute bastard" (Sloboda 2011, 141), and at the same time that of the "sacred clown" embodying paradoxical expressions of "sanctification, profanity, stupidity, menace and mirth" (Van Ham 2009, 318). Coupland (2011) argues that virtuoso performance in punk is not simply about the absence of virtuosity, or "bad popular music," but rather it has a quality of "ephemeral performative transgression" infused with a political agenda, and that Rotten's on-stage self was "fully contiguous with his off-stage self."

Among the fans of the Sex Pistols was an outrageous group of young punks known as the Bromley Contingent, named after the district of South London that they came from. The Bromley Contingent included Siouxsie Sioux and Steve Severin, who would soon form Siouxsie and the Banshees; Billy Idol, who would join punk band Chelsea and then Generation X; and well-known punks Soo Catwoman and Jordan. They were described as "a posse of unrepentant poseurs, committed to attaining fame despite the paucity of talent other than being noticed; achieving their aim by displaying themselves in a manner meticulously calculated to kill" (Burchill and Parsons 1987).

Punk came more slowly to the rest of the United Kingdom. There would be a delay of approximately one year between what was happening in London and similar occurrences in the rest of the country, and when punk did arrive, it was quite different. This was a much more DIY scene, and at least at first, it was not distinct from the established rock scene. Small groupings started to develop, helped by the emergence of local bands. The Sex Pistols actually played relatively few concerts outside of London. However, the importance of those few gigs cannot be underestimated. Early Pistols gigs were life changing for a small number of people, and shocking and annoying to others. Yet the truth was that those gigs also remained largely insignificant to most people. Punk in the provinces had a number of specific characteristics (Cobley 1999). Punk gigs were often dangerous and marred by violence, as local camps saw them as opportunities for fights between themselves and the security staff, who were either denying them entry or preventing them from getting close to their heroes. The links to local "politics" are very clear. Other characteristics include the DIY and bricolage nature of punk dress. The importance of local venues as rallying points and for providing the opportunity to experience punk rock is evident, as is the importance of local bands such as the Buzzcocks in the North West and Penetration in the North East, and particular gigs as "events," which served to develop punk culture.

In July 1976, two new punk bands, The Clash and The Damned, showed up as support acts for the Sex Pistols. Things were starting to happen and the scene was starting to make waves across the United Kingdom. Punk culture was being born.

2

SUMMER AND AUTUMN 1976

SOMEONE'S GOT to come along and say to all of us, "All your ideas about rock and roll, all your ideas about sound, all your ideas about guitars, all your ideas about this and that are a load of wank. This is where it is!" . . . Someone's got to come along and say, "F**k you."
—*Alex Harvey, November 1973*

The summer of 1976 was one of the hottest on record in the United Kingdom, with a heat wave that lasted for weeks. The British people basked in the sunshine, and it became so hot there was a drought and the use of garden hoses was banned. That summer was, however, memorable for a number of other reasons. In the Irish Republic, a state of emergency had been declared prior to the introduction of antiterrorist legislation. More than twenty-thousand women, both Protestant and Catholic, marched for peace in Northern Ireland. British industry was in the grip of strong unions that called the workers out on seemingly endless strikes; there were power cuts across the country, which was still recovering from the effects of inflation and a recession. The Labour Party promised much to the people, yet little seemed to have changed for the average working-class person. For many young people Britain was a cold, miserable place with little promise of employment. The old way wasn't working and young people felt powerless over their future. Per Lydon, "The germ, the seed of the Sex Pistols generated from that. . . . The Sex Pistols should have happened and did" (Temple 2000). The Sex Pistols and punk were about to provide young people with the power they were so desperately seeking.

Punk was breaking ground, particularly in London, and the Sex Pistols continued to play exciting and exhilarating concerts in the capital and farther afield. The music press in the United Kingdom was starting to pick on the new rock sensation, and New Musical Express was beginning to champion the Pistols' cause. In the United States in May, the new wave movement was also growing. The Ramones played two nights at the Bottom Line in New York City, tearing through a twenty-minute set of lightning-quick rock songs with titles such as "Beat on the Brat" and "Now I Wanna Sniff some Glue," all of which started with Dee Dee Ramone shouting "One, Two, Three, Faw." In Europe, the first European Punk Rock Festival was staged at Mont de Marsa, near Bordeaux, France. The bill featured The Damned, Count Bishops, Pink Fairies, Eddie and the Hot Rods, and the Hammersmith Gorillas. Future Pretender front person Chrissie Hynde was in London, having arrived in 1973 from the United States. She "couldn't believe it when she first came here: the dole, the NHS (National Health Service), squatters' rights" (Murison 2015, 12). She would soon be drawn into the world of sex, punk, and the Sex Pistols (Hynde 2015).

Musically, the old rock music guard continued as if nothing was happening. The Rolling Stones played to two hundred thousand people in Knebworth Park on a hot August night, while Queen played a free concert in Hyde Park. Elton John and Kiki Dee hit number 1 in the UK singles charts for six weeks. Elvis was visited by Elton John at a concert in the Capitol Centre, in Largo, Maryland. Thin Lizzy entered the UK and US charts with their massive rock anthem "The Boys are Back in Town." Heavy rock band Deep Purple announced they were splitting up. If you were to look at the UK singles chart you wouldn't have noticed any difference from that of previous years. On June 27, 1976, you could choose from Liverpool soul group The Real Thing at number 1 with "You to Me are Everything," TV show talent contest winners Our Kid at number 2 with "You Just Might See Me Cry," Rod Stewart at number 5 with "Tonight's the Night," and Paul McCartney and Wings at number 10 with "Silly Love Songs." But the kids hanging around the street corners and going to gigs in ballrooms and clubs in London were living in a different world, listening to a different beat, and ready for something authentic, raw, exciting, and relevant to *them*. The old guard were boring "old farts," dinosaurs. What they needed was a new kind of band. A band that looked like them, sang songs with lyrics that talked in the same language as them, and cared about the same everyday things. A band that they could go and see for less than a pound, and who understood them and knew about the things that concerned them. They were tired of stars who were getting further and further from their reach.

THE SONGS WERE STARTING TO DEVELOP

In July 1976, the Pistols began to record demos that drew from their growing song catalog. They had assembled a strong set of self-penned punk rock classics and covers that displayed their musical influences. These were the songs that they were performing live on a regular basis, and that were becoming firm favorites of their growing number of fans. Although these songs had yet to be released on vinyl, or played on the radio, they were well known by Pistols devotees, who were beginning to sing along with every word that Rotten snarled. The same songs were to become tracks on their debut album and, in some cases, future hit singles.

"Did You No Wrong" is one of their very early songs and had originally been written by Wally Nightingale. "Submission" started out as a concept of McLaren's; his intention being for his boys to write a song about submission in a sadomasochistic context. Instead, they decided to disregard McLaren's wishes and, as a bit of fun, write a silly poppy song about a submarine mission.

There is some debate as to the origin and meaning of the song "Satellite." Some believe it to simply be about the satellite towns around London, such as High Wycombe, Welwyn Garden City, and Watford. Others (e.g., the punk77.co.uk website) claim that it was written by Rotten about his girlfriend at the time, Shanne Bradley, who was in the Nipple Erectors (a.k.a. the Nips) with (soon to be Pogues frontman) Shane MacGowan, who lived in St. Albans, a "satellite" town.

"New York" is a parody of, and rant about, New York new wave bands in general ("an imitation from New York . . . you put on a bad show . . . you think it's swell playing Max's Kansas . . ."), drugs ("still out on those pills"), and the New York Dolls in particular. It was also a chance to get at Malcolm and his love of the United States, with Dolls attitude and swagger thrown in for good measure.

"I'm a Lazy Sod" (which became "Seventeen") portrays the lives of teenage punks ("we like noise . . . we don't care about long hairs, I don't wear flares.") and their lazy, meaningless existence. It was apparently written about John's friend and soon-to-be bandmate, Sid Vicious. Similarly, "No Feelings" is a rock 'n' roll ballad about a selfish, narcissistic young punk ("I'm in love with myself, my beautiful self"). "Pretty Vacant," in a similar vein, is an anthem of teenage apathy, painting a picture of youth who see their future as bleak, and as a result feel there is no point in trying to do anything constructive to change things: "we're pretty vacant" and "we don't care." "Problems" is a great rock song that further explores the punk ethic and dilemma: "the problem is you!"

"Flowers of Romance" is an early song that was never recorded, although a few live recordings exist. This song was quite different from others in the set and would consist of Rotten screaming, "Flowers . . . Woodstock," over a discordant slow dirge of thrashing guitars and feedback. It was a hint of what Lydon's music was to develop into in his post-Pistols band Public Image Limited (PiL). The name "Flowers of Romance" was also given, by Rotten, to an early punk band that featured Sid Vicious and Viv Albertine of the Slits. The title would turn up again a few years later as a PiL song and album moniker.

These songs were a manifesto of UK punk. Fast, loud, in-your-face thrash rock 'n' roll that charged along underneath Rotten's snarling, sneering lyrics. The lyrics told the story of disaffected youth, sitting in their bedrooms, lost with no job, no hope, no future, and no one to speak for them. Enter Johnny Rotten and the Sex Pistols, charging in and giving these young people a cause, a spokesperson, and loud, raucous music and crazy live performances that they could lose themselves in.

The cover songs that the Pistols were playing at the time had been chosen for a number of reasons. Some of the tracks had been played since the early days, before Rotten joined. These were mod and pop songs chosen by Glen or Steve and reflected the songs they were listening to and their early influences. Rotten focused on particular phrases in these songs, changed the words around, and snarled them out. "Want you to know that I care" in the Small Faces' "Whatcha Gonna Do About It" became "Want you to know I *don't* care." Others drew from early punk and garage rock.

"(I'm Not Your) Steppin' Stone" is a basic garage band rock song written by Tommy Boyce and Bobby Hart. It was originally recorded by US pop rock band Paul Revere and the Raiders in 1966, and was a hit for the Monkees later that same year. It is likely that the Pistols were familiar with the Monkees' version of the song, which was the B side of their number 1 hit "I'm a Believer." It was a poppy tune, which may have been chosen for the band by Glen.

The Dave Berry song "Don't Gimme No Lip Child" is a driving R&B song, and was also originally a B side, having been coupled with Berry's 1964 big hit "The Crying Game." It provided a great vehicle for chugging chords from Steve. The Iggy Pop song "No Fun" appeared on the Stooges' 1969 debut album, which music journalist Will Hodgkinson (2006, 203) describes as "charged and brutal garage-rock." This song offered Rotten the opportunity to snarl the lyrics in "snot-nosed defiance" (Ward 1969).

The Who's "Substitute" and the Small Faces' "Whatcha Gonna Do About It" were perhaps more obvious, and certainly better known, song choices. Both are charged pop rock mod classics. Steve Marriott and Ronnie Lane's "Whatcha Gonna Do About It" was the Small Faces' debut single and peaked at number 14 in the UK charts, staying on the chart for a total of fourteen weeks. The Pistols (or rather, Johnny Rotten) changed the lyrics of one line from "I want you to know that I *love* you baby" to "I want you to know that I *hate* you baby." They would also sometimes play a cover of the Small Faces' "Understanding," which was the B side of their number 1 hit "All or Nothing." "Substitute" was written by Who guitarist Pete Townshend and released as a single in 1966, reaching number 5 in the UK charts. The song was a big favorite of The Who and their fans, and was almost always featured in their live concerts. It was apparently influenced by the Tamla Motown classic "The Tracks of My Tears" by Smokey Robinson and the Miracles. The line of that song "Although she may be cute she's just a substitute" was apparently obsessed by Townshend that he "decided to celebrate the word with a song all its own" (*Rolling Stone* 2005). In the hands of the Sex Pistols, "Substitute" became a vehicle for Rotten's sneering sarcasm.

PERFORMING

The band continued to play gigs around the United Kingdom with mixed success. Hasham (2015) wrote of their gig at Nottingham Boat Club in August 1976: "It's been said that when they played Manchester the same year, everyone in the audience went out and formed bands. When they played Nottingham, alas, everybody went out to the chip shop and got the last bus home." However, they were creating a reaction in most places they played. Sometimes that reaction was negative, sometimes positive, but there was always a reaction. "We managed to offend all the people we were f***ing fed up with," said Lydon (Temple 2000).

High drama occurred at a Sex Pistols performance in 1976. Per Sid Vicious, Rotten was "incredible, unbelievable," and an "anti-star" on stage (Temple 2000); a pure bundle of energy, a force of nature. Their performance contained elements of music hall, theater, and the great British comedians. In the movie *The Filth and the Fury*, Lydon compares elements of his performance to the playfulness of Arthur Askey, the silly "tattifelarius" fun of Ken Dodd, and the pathos of Norman Wisdom. There was also a sense of danger; you felt that anything could happen. Rotten was as frightening as he was funny; his stare could burn through you and was to be avoided. He was using clothes to help define the style, persona, and concept; he would be dressed in a mix of home-made items with tears, safety pins, and painted-on slogans, and the more fashionable yet equally outrageous and shocking gear from the stock of McLaren and Westwood's shop, SEX.

The band had argued among themselves from the very first day that they all came together and tensions between them only added to the drama of their performance. Each member had a different reason for being on stage. John was starting to form, and believe in, the Pistols concept of being an agent of change; a reaction to the situation that young people were in, and to what they were feeling. Glen wanted to be a pop star, to get a hit single in the charts, and appear on *Top of the Pops*. Steve just enjoyed the attention, and looking for girls, and Paul enjoyed drinking and crashing on those drums. Malcolm tried to use and manipulate the boys and the tensions between them, playing them against each other. He saw them as his own piece of performance art, a "sculpture," his "little artful dodgers" (Temple 2000).

The audience was gradually changing. A growing body of fans across the country was getting their hair cut short, swapping their flares for drainpipe jeans, and making their own clothes. Punk was giving them a focus, a reason to get up, go out, and meet, something to listen to, talk about, and a lifestyle around and within which they could craft a new sense of purpose, meaning, and identity.

"The essence, I think, of the relationship between us and our audience is the same thing exactly as the Dolls. The Pistols don't play great and as such, a kid in the audience can relate to that. He can think 'Yeah, I can possibly play that.' There's that proximity. A kid can visualise himself being up there on stage. Kids can't relate to Led Zeppelin; all those barriers, big auditoriums . . . ridiculous. It's got out of hand" (Malcolm McLaren, interviewed by Nick Kent, *Sounds*, 1976a).

THE SCREEN ON THE GREEN CONCERT, AUGUST 29, 1976

The Screen on the Green is a movie theater on Islington Green in London. It is one of the oldest continuously running theaters in the United Kingdom. On Sunday, August 29, 1976, the Screen on the Green was host to a "Midnight Special" concert organized as a showcase for the Sex Pistols and the growing punk scene. The Sex Pistols were supported by two new punk bands: The Clash and the Buzzcocks. The concert is one of the earliest known (along with the Manchester Free Trade Hall concert of June 1976) recorded performance by the Sex Pistols.

The concert was a rallying point for the new punk movement and was attended by aficionados decked out in their most outrageous, and largely homemade, gear. This was the first big showcase concert in the capital, and as a result, it received significant coverage in the national music press, with both *Sounds* and *New Musical Express* reporting on the gig. The Bromley contingent were out in force, with Siouxsie wearing a leather bondage top that left her breasts fully exposed. In between the bands the film *Scorpio Rising* was shown. *Scorpio Rising* is a 1963 experimental short film by Kenneth Anger, with themes of the occult, biker subculture, homosexuality, Catholicism, and Nazism set against a soundtrack of 1960s rock music. *Scorpio Rising* is considered by some to be the first drama film to feature a rock 'n' roll soundtrack. When the film was first screened in Los Angeles, the American Nazi Party protested that it insulted their flag. The police were called in and the film's run was canceled.

This was The Clash's third gig and their performance at the time was fast garage rock. They were led by Joe Strummer, who would spit out politically charged lyrics of songs like "I'm So Bored with the USA," "White Riot" ("I wanna riot, a riot of my own"), and "London's Burning." Strummer had been a member of pub rock band the 101ers. The Clash were soon seen as contenders for the Pistols' throne and one of the most relevant and important bands of the punk era.

The Sex Pistols came on stage in the early hours of the morning, opening with some audience abuse from Johnny Rotten, which was a normal way of starting their concerts at the time. They played a blistering set and won over more fans that night. Charles Shaar Murray, reporting the gig in the *New Musical Express* (1976), declared that "any halfway competent rock and roll pulse-fingerer knows that this is The Year Of The Punk" and warned his readers, "You wanted Sex Pistols and now you've got 'em. Trouble is, they look like they aren't going to go away, so what are you going to do with them? Alternatively—ha ha— what are they going to do with *you*?" He wrote of the Pistols:

> any reports that I had heard and that you may have heard about the Pistols being lame and sloppy are completely and utterly full of s°°t. They play loud, clean and tight and they don't mess around. . . . They have the same air of seething just-about-repressed violence that the Feelgoods have [Dr. Feelgood was one of the leading pub rock bands of the time, and seen by many as a forerunner of the punk movement]. . . . The first thirty seconds of their set blew out all the boring, amateurish artsy-fartsy mock-decadence that preceded it purely by virtue of its tautness, directness and utter realism. "Should I say all the trendy fings like 'peace and love,' maaaaaaan?" asked Johnny Rotten, leaning out off the stage manically jerking off his retractable mike-stand. "Are you all having a good time, maaaaaaan?" Believe it: this *ain't* the summer of love.

"Launched in a blaze of smoke bombs, it is their best gig yet, Steve raging away in simultaneous feedback, noise and ringing, crystal clear rhythms, Paul and Glen thundering like a stampeding herd of cattle. John knocks a capped tooth out with the mike during the second song.

The blinding pain provokes an unbelievable performance" (Ingham 1976). The Screen on the Green gig was an important marker in the development of the Sex Pistols' career and in the growth of the new UK punk movement.

CHELMSFORD PRISON, SEPTEMBER 17, 1976

The Sex Pistols continued to play gigs around London and across the country. Malcolm McLaren searched for opportunities where the band could play in unusual venues. In September, the Sex Pistols performed to around five hundred inmates at Chelmsford prison, a Category B prison in Essex. Category B prisons are for those who do not require maximum security, but for whom escape still needs to be made very difficult. The prisoners are, in general, serving sentences of three years and up. The Sex Pistols weren't the first band to perform in a prison, of course: as Johnny Cash explained, "The culture of a thousand years is shattered with the clanging of the cell door behind you. Life outside behind you immediately becomes unreal. You begin to not care that it exists. All you have with you in the cell is your bare animal instincts" (liner notes; Johnny Cash 1968). This concert was booked as a normal gig by McLaren; apparently the prison held regular monthly concerts by up-and-coming bands.

The prisoners were confused by the crashing racket that came out of the band that night. The concert coincided with Paul Cook's last day as an apprentice at Watney's brewery; he had just quit his job to go professional. Paul had been drinking with workmates and arrived after the rest of the band, a little worse for wear. During the performance he fell off his drum stool, much to the amusement of the rest of the band. Johnny Rotten was wearing a T-shirt with "NO FUTURE" on the front and "ANARCHY" across the back. The gig took place in the prison's small concert theater. They warmed up by playing a cover of the Small Faces' "Wham Bam Thank You Mam." The prisoners arrived. "They run. Long hair, short hair, young, middle aged, their clothes a jumble of jackets, sweaters, slippers, boots. Six blacks stroll in; five of them walk out after ten minutes. Some guys have sewn flares into their Levis" (Terry 1976).

"God, there won't be any girls in the audience," said Steve. "That's alright," jeered road manager Nils, "You'll still be able to play."

The Pistols started with "Anarchy in the UK." John taunted the audience: "You're like a bunch of f***ing statues! I bet you've all got a good case of piles! Move!" "We're not allowed to" was the response. John continued: "I don't care—tear the f***ing place apart!" A recording of the gig was subsequently released as a bootleg LP, complete with dialogue overdubbed by producer Dave Goodman, which was designed to make it sound like Johnny Rotten was inciting a riot.

"'You're all stupid, you got caught. Better do your homework next time. . . . I bet you like it here, it's just like being in the womb, i'nt it? . . . .' What could be more punk than a bunch of, well, 'punks,' playing for a group of caged human animals that are this close to tearing them apart, and relishing the opportunity? Clearly, this isn't Johnny Cash's prison crowd; by the sound of it, these guys are out for BLOOD! As the set fades out, you wonder exactly HOW the band managed to get out of there un-shivved!" (totheleftofwest 2008). According to Dave Goodman, "the band ended up to thunderous applause."

THE 100 CLUB PUNK SPECIAL, SEPTEMBER 21 AND 22, 1976

The 100 Club Punk Special (often referred to as the first punk festival) was a two-day event held at the 100 Club in London. The 100 Club had been a venue for jazz until it became the home of punk rock in the summer of 1976. The Sex Pistols had a residency at the club and played there on nine occasions between March and August of 1976. Their tenth appearance at the 100 Club was as part of the Punk Special in September 1976. The event featured eight bands that were associated with the rapidly growing UK punk rock music scene.

The lineup of the Punk Special was:

- Monday, September 20: Subway Sect, Siouxsie and the Banshees, The Clash, the Sex Pistols
- Tuesday, September 21: Stinky Toys, The Vibrators (featuring Chris Spedding), The Damned, the Buzzcocks

The concert was a significant watershed for the UK punk movement and received much publicity in the music press. This was the point at which the punk movement began to move out of the underground and into the mainstream. The bands were all new and several were playing together for the first time. Subway Sect was formed by Vic Goddard and a group of soul fans who had been going to see the Pistols. Joe Strummer of The Clash declared, "Number One for me at the moment are the Subway Sect. They've got some good ideas" (Bendel 2015).

Siouxsie Sioux, along with fellow Bromley fan Steve Severin, decided it was time to put together a band. For the 100 Club gig, they rapidly assembled a group consisting of Siouxsie on vocals, Severin on bass, Sid Vicious (who would go on to join the Sex Pistols) on drums, and Marco Pirroni (who would join the Models and then Adam and the Ants) on guitar. Their set was completely improvisational. They didn't have any songs, so Siouxsie recited "The Lord's Prayer" over a thrash of punk noise and discord.

The Clash were seen, along with The Damned and Eddie and the Hot Rods, as the contenders for the Pistols' crown. Formed by Joe Strummer, Mick Jones, and Paul Simone, The Clash were taking their music and attitude seriously and had been rehearsing solidly for a month prior to the 100 Club gig. Their music was fast thrash overlaid with lyrics with political overtones. The Clash had already opened for the Sex Pistols in April 1976. "I knew something was up," Strummer explained. "I went out in the crowd which was fairly sparse. And I saw the future—with a snotty handkerchief—right in front of me. It was immediately clear. Pub rock was, 'Hello, you bunch of drunks, I'm gonna play these boogies and I hope you like them.' The Pistols came out . . . and their attitude was 'Here's our tunes, and we couldn't give a flying f°°k whether you like them or not. In fact, we're gonna play them even if you f°°king hate them'" (interview in *Record Collector*, Strummer, 2000).

Stinky Toys were a French band who had come over to London especially for the event. The Vibrators were a new punk group who backed guitarist Chis Spedding at the festival. Spedding had recently been in the charts with his single "Motor Bikin'" and was an important figure in the development of UK punk rock, producing some of the Sex Pistols early demos. He apparently taught The Vibrators a few songs in the dressing room before going on stage. Ron Watts states, "None of the shows were rehearsed. It was just people, getting up and trying to do something" (Watts 2006).

The Damned would be the first punk band to release a single, "New Rose," and their set at the time also included a manic version of The Beatles' "Help" and some embryonic versions of songs that would feature on their first album. Van Ham (2009) compares several of the early punks to "clowns"; The Damned were certainly moving in that direction, building an image that blended gothic horror (Gunn, 1999) with lunacy and vaudeville. Caroline Coon (1982) describes Captain Sensible as having "a front as benevolently mad as a village idiot's. The Buzzcocks were much more poppy and were already developing tunes with strong hooks that would soon see them in the charts with singles like "What Do I Get?" and "Ever Fallen in Love (with someone you shouldn't've)."

"You get the feeling at Pistols gigs that everyone's posing so they can't really be punks can they? Punks are carefree, and I mean completely . . . you know, like a football [soccer] fan who kicks in someone's head and don't care a s**t. Yet, the Pistols crowd are not punks, they're too vain. But what's wrong with that so am I" (Perry 1976).

Sometime around this time, the "pogo" dance started. It consisted of throwing yourself up and down in the air, jumping furiously along with the fast beat of the music. Sid Vicious is often credited with being the originator of the pogo. In the movie *The Filth and the Fury* he claims to have invented it to annoy the Bromley contingent, who he "hated," by creating a dance that enabled him to charge around the dance floor crashing into them.

Sadly, the festival was, perhaps predictably, marred by outbreaks of violence. On the first night, it was interrupted when fights broke out. Things got worse the following night with an even nastier outbreak of violence when at least three people needed hospital treatment and a few were arrested. A glass was thrown, reportedly by Sid Vicious, which shattered and injured a girl's eye. As a result, the 100 Club decided to ban punk bands from appearing at the venue, thus reducing even further the number of venues in London where the new groups could perform.

The event was attended by many people who were to become involved in the punk scene, including Shane MacGowan (later of the Pogues), Viv Albertine (of the Slits), Chrissie Hynde (the Pretenders),

Gaye Advert and T.V. Smith (the Adverts), and Susan Carrington (who would soon open The Roxy, an important London punk club).

> the audience stretches around the block. As the band hit the stage there is a mass epidemic of pogo-dancing. John looks at the seething crowd with a satisfied grin: "Great." As the evening progresses the band tread a thinner and thinner line between order and chaos. The encore of "Anarchy" is a blazing carnage of feedback, noise and head crushing rhythm. It is great. (Ingham 1976)

THE CHÂLET DU LAC, PARIS, SEPTEMBER 3 AND 5, 1976

In September, the Sex Pistols played two concerts at the Châlet du Lac in Paris; their first concerts abroad. Believing that everything happens in Paris, Malcolm McLaren was keen to book a show for the band in the French capital, and the Pistols were equally keen to play there. Malcolm had managed to cement a good deal with French promoter Pierre Bénain, who paid the band £1,000 plus hotel and plane tickets. The Châlet du Lac was a disco club that was re-opening after major refurbishment, and its owners were very excited to be able to feature the most fashionable new English rock band of the time for the special opening event.

Around two thousand people attended the first concert on September 3. The Bromley contingent drove to the shows to offer their support. Hermann Schwartz (guitar player with Metal Urbain) tells that "the place was very hot. A lot of Johnny Hallyday's fans in black leather jackets were here looking for trouble. Some of them carried boiled potatoes with razor blades inside their pocket—it was a good way to slash somebody at the time" (Geant-Vert 2009).

It had taken some time to get the Pistols' equipment through customs, and it arrived just one hour before the band took to the stage. There was no time for a sound check and Dave Goodman's solution was to turn the volume up full. The Sex Pistols came on stage at midnight and went straight into "Anarchy in the U.K." The sound was deafening. Rotten was dressed especially for the occasion in an outrageous bondage suit complete with crucifixes, swastikas, and safety pins. The newly refurbished venue featured a classy glass stage and red laser beams criss-crossed the Pistols as they performed. The audience was largely made up of disco fans and most of those present were simply astonished by what they witnessed. Riton (Angel Face): "I was an MC5 fan but the beginning of the show impressed me a lot. The sound, the look, etc. . . . All was perfect—and I even hated French punks! After a few songs I was closer to the bar tender than the band, but what a f**king show! The sound was incredible: loud and clear. The exact opposite of the French bands" (Geant-Vert 2009).

Caroline Coon said, "But as most of the audience recovered from their shock and exploded into a wild display of rock 'n' roll dancing, the band, encouraged by this show of approval, took off. The atmosphere was now a freaky combination of unrestrained enjoyment and intense hatred. The band's effect on Paris was as controversial, but as stimulating, as in London. Young Parisians are as frustrated with the state of rock as their English counterparts" (Coon 1976).

Less than one week after the Paris gigs, I was lucky enough to see the Sex Pistols myself for the first time. The concert was poorly attended and took place in the White Horse Inn, Whitby, in the North East of England on September 11, 1976. I thought the Pistols were amazing, although the rest of the crowd was less impressed. There was a beautiful, ramshackle amateurishness about their performance that night, and for me it was all about Johnny Rotten. His performance was authentic, raw, innocent, dangerous, alarming; it was as if he was driven by a chaotic and manic passion. And his eyes, his stare, burnt through me. Although many of the people in the audience were simply shocked and outraged, others such as Noble (Abitoftap), who commented about the gig on my blog, were affected in a different way: "I was there [Whitby] in '76 . . . great night. I was only 15 got in through a bouncer that was my brother's best friend, a teacher at my school told us about them, it was a life changing experience they were raw loud and exiting, it was the best time to be a teenager ever. I saw them lots of times since" (Abitoftap, in Smith 2015). Others were simply there for a drink and a Saturday night out. "There was a guy who promoted there . . . mainly the disco but with bands as well, usually '60s veterans . . . place was vile . . . locals getting drunk v quickly, sick in the corners and fights most weeks. It was always on the verge of being closed down. My younger brother saw them but can't remember . . . he was there for the drink . . . although he did recall seeing them wandering along the pier the next day" (Abitoftap, in Smith 2015).

EMI

In October, the Sex Pistols caught the attention of and signed to major record label EMI. There had been a lot of discussion in the media as to which record label might sign the band, and it was clear that they, and McLaren in particular, were hanging out for the best possible offer. Some of the big labels were keen to sign the band; others less so. Rumor has it that McLaren was literally thrown out of the CBS office while the band waited outside in a car. There was also an argument that a band such as the Sex Pistols should stay true to their ideals and sign to a smaller, independent label, in the same way that fellow punk band The Damned had signed to Stiff Records. However, the lure of the big label won out in the end. McLaren and his boys were attracted by the money and the exposure that a large, established label could offer. Other contenders were Chrysalis (the band was said to hate the label's butterfly logo, according to Southall [2007]), RAK Records (which was home to UK chart-toppers Mud and Suzi Quatro), and Polydor. In the end, a two-year deal was signed quite quickly (at McLaren's insistence) and was set to give the Sex Pistols £40,000 over two years, on the condition that they provided two albums.

The signing was widely reported in the UK mainstream and music press, and there was some surprise that a punk band claiming to be about anarchy had chosen to align themselves with a stuffy pillar of the establishment, such as EMI. However, the move fitted with McLaren's strategy, presumably to work from inside and use established institutions to chip away and destroy "the system." Johnny Rotten declared, "We've got the best. We wouldn't have signed with a crackpot little company. Now we can't be ignored" (*Melody Maker* 1976).

Now that the band was signed, discussion focused on what song would be their first single. McLaren and the band were insistent that "Anarchy in the U.K." have that honor; they felt it their strongest song, and it would also give a clear message of intention to the public. These guys were out to create anarchy, and they wanted to proudly tell everyone. The EMI executives favored "Pretty Vacant," which they felt was a catchier tune and more likely chart material. In the end, the Pistols won out, and it was agreed that "Anarchy" would be the first single, followed by "Pretty Vacant" and then an album. This was the traditional starting point for a new band. Preparations were also starting to be put in place for their first major UK tour, which was also going to be called "Anarchy in the U.K." and was to call at major concert halls across the country.

Meanwhile, the Pistols were continuing to play small gigs, including shows at Cleopatra's in Derby; Strikes Club, Stoke; Dundee College in Scotland, and Lafayette Club in Wolverhampton. In between gigs, they were in the studio recording tracks for their debut album with producer Dave Goodman. The results were raw energy. "The idea was to get the spirit of the live performance" (Savage 2005, 177). However, EMI had other ideas and brought in producer Chris Thomas to record new versions of the tracks. Thomas came with a strong, more traditional rock pedigree, having produced Roxy Music and Pink Floyd's *Dark Side of the Moon*.

ANARCHY IN THE U.K.

"Anarchy in the U.K." was released on November 26, 1977, on EMI Records in an iconic plain black sleeve. This piece of 7-inch vinyl signaled a call to arms for England's disenchanted youth. In one perfect piece of pop, the Sex Pistols' first single set out a manifesto that young people around the world felt, understood, and embraced. It is easy to underestimate just how influential and important this record was; in 3 minutes and 31 seconds, it captured the mood, feelings, and hopes of a generation, and challenged them to dare to initiate their own revolution.

In one single piece of pure, raw rock 'n' roll, "Anarchy" fuses Steve Jones' classic slamming rock chords with Johnny Rotten's sneering, searing vocals. The Sex Pistols simply, and effortlessly, blew away everything that came before them and set the bar for those who followed. In "Anarchy," the Sex Pistols set out a vision of destruction of the old and the downfall of government, with the promise of freedom and the independence of self-rule, focusing and releasing their fans' anger through the snarling, spitting vocals of Johnny Rotten. The song uses clever play on words, designed to shock; the song's opening statement is: "I am an antichrist, I am an anarchist"; the rhyme is somewhat forced, yet it works. The line "I use the NME" purposely confounds the words "NME" and "Enemy," where "the NME" is the British music magazine

New Musical Express. The song ends with Rotten urging us to "Get pissed. . . . Destroy!"

Rotten had apparently started the song by writing the first line as "I am an anti-Christ" as a shocking opening statement. He then need something to rhyme with this and came up with "I am an anarchist," which he snarled accordingly to force the rhyme. It was all about attitude and the power of the message. This wasn't a happy pop song; it was a sneering, charging punk rock anthem in the making, designed to shock, energize, infuriate, and empower.

In "Anarchy," the Sex Pistols and their manager Malcolm McLaren set out to deliberately cause controversy. The record reached number 38 on the UK singles charts, and the punk rock movement began to gain steam. In 2004, *Rolling Stone* magazine placed "Anarchy" at number 56 in their 500 Greatest Songs of All Time, declaring: "This is what the beginning of a revolution sounds like: an explosion of punk-rock guitar noise and Johnny Rotten's evil cackle. The Sex Pistols set out to become a national scandal in the U.K., and they succeeded with their debut single. Jones made his guitar sound like a pub brawl, while Rotten snarled, spat, snickered and ended the song by urging his fans, 'Get pissed/Destroy!'"

Rotten later said in *Mojo* (2008) magazine: "It flowed quite naturally . . . you can't ever underestimate the sheer driving energy poverty will bring . . . being denied everything and access to everything." Bassist Glen Matlock (also in *Mojo* 2008): "Everything about it is just right. It's one of those rare moments captured, the vibe, the groove."

"Anarchy" was banned from the radio in the United Kingdom yet reached number 38 in the UK singles charts before being withdrawn by EMI as a result of the furor around the Sex Pistols' appearance on the Bill Grundy show, which is discussed in full in the next chapter. The song is now regarded as the definitive anthem of punk rock and had a massive impact at the time of its release. "It sounded like nothing that had come before and unleashed the Pistols to a wider audience. An audience probably more used to chart toppers like Showaddywaddy and Abba! Things would never be the same again" (Sex Pistols Official Website 2018).

"Anarchy in the U.K." was not the first punk single to be released by a British band. That honor went to The Damned and "New Rose" or possibly The Vibrators and "We Vibrate." However, those singles were straight-on rock 'n' roll, while "Anarchy" introduced a new political attitude and came with a loud and clear message for the youth of the day.

Punk was gaining ground, and "Anarchy in the UK" created a focus for the new movement. A chance encounter on a television program would move things to an entirely different level.

3

THE BILL GRUNDY INCIDENT

Autumn of 1976 started off uneventfully. Certainly in terms of music, little had changed. Punk may have been gathering a grassroots following, but to most people it was either a small blip in music fashion, or something that they were totally unaware of. One look at the charts and you would think that punk simply wasn't happening. The old guard was very much in evidence. Indeed, the UK singles chart was seriously middle of the road. In mid-November, the number 1 singles spot was held by Chicago with "If You Leave Me Now" and also featured Leo Sayer, rock 'n' roll revivalists Showaddywaddy, The Who with a rere-cording of "Subsititute," and Greek crooner Demis Roussos with "When Forever Has Gone." The only hint of punk was the appearance of Eddie and the Hot Rods, who were at the time considered a serious rival to the Sex Pistols, at number 37 with their song "Teenage Depression." The album chart didn't read like this was the year of the emergence of punk rock. The number 1 albums of the year so far were by Perry Como, Queen, Roy Orbison, Slim Whitman, the soundtrack of the musical *Rock Follies*, Status Quo, Led Zeppelin, ABBA, Rod Stewart, the Beach Boys, the Stylistics, Bert Weedon, and Glen Campbell. The only hint that something was happening in terms of new wave music was signified by the presence of Dr. Feelgood's *Stupidity* in the chart, which held the number 1 spot for one week in October 1976.

Punk was starting to appear on our TV screens, however. The inno-vative British journalist and TV presenter Janet Street-Porter was mak-ing a name for herself exploring topics and cultural trends that her contemporaries were ignoring or even dismissing. On November 22, 1976, *The London Weekend Show* broadcast Street-Porter's documentary titled "Punk," which featured interviews with the Sex Pistols, Clash (before they became known as "The" Clash), and Siouxsie Sioux. Lucky, and probably slightly bemused, viewers also got to see the Pistols play "Pretty Vacant," "Submission," "Anarchy in the U.K.," and "No Fun." The Pistols had been filmed playing live at Notre Dame Hall, London. This was the first television show to take punk to the masses. Things were starting to happen.

With such a predictable array of artists capturing the attention and mood of the British public, it was clear that it was time for a long overdue shake-up. We had experienced much culture change during the 1960s, but so far the 1970s hadn't taken up the strands of freedom, liberation, and revolution that emerged during the previous decade. Young people wanted something to happen, something that was their own, and something that would start to shake the establishment in the same way that their older brothers and sisters had. They were hungry for change and were willing something to happen. The Sex Pistols instinctively felt and embodied this, and through one almost coincidental episode they were about to provide young people with the jolt that they were waiting for.

BUSINESS AS USUAL

The Sex Pistols continued to gig across the country, playing to small crowds that were gathering largely out of curiosity as a result of reports of the punk phenomenon that was appearing in the music and national press. On November 29, 1976, they played at Lanchester Polytechnic Students' Union in Coventry supported by The Clash. This event was reported in the national press, largely because of the reaction of the students' union entertainments manager. The students at Lanchester Polytechnic were used to seeing progressive rock bands play at their dances and weren't prepared for punk rock. David Parker, who attended the Pistols gig, remembers that the first band he saw at Lanchester Polytechnic were Welsh rockers Man, followed by the progressive rock outfit Renaissance. The bass player in Renaissance wore an embroidered cape, which tells you a lot about the sort of band they were. At the time, concerts in clubs consisted of long-haired hippie types (and I include myself in that description) sitting cross-legged on the floor listening to Led Zeppelin and Pink Floyd.

The concert was only half-capacity with students and locals going along largely out of curiosity to experience the new punk rock music that they had been reading about in the music papers. Photographs from the gig show that Rotten wore a torn black plastic top and Steve Jones a black bondage shirt and leather trousers. David Parker remembers that the Pistols were very loud and the "physical power of the volume and thinking that they sounded absolutely amazing." He recalls them opening and closing the set with "Anarchy in the U.K." and that there were thirty or forty people in attendance, including only two or three dressed as punks, and looking very conspicuous. The band "blasted their way through a dozen or so numbers in a tightly-knit and professional manner—much in contrast to the lurid tales of fights and gobbing on the audience that had started to emerge from the London scene." David came away from the gig "highly impressed and with my ears ringing" and thought that "the Sex Pistols were great!" (Parker 1976).

Kevin and Lynda Harrison, soon to front the Coventry band Urge, were at the concert: "When the Pistols got on stage and started up the riff from 'Pretty Vacant,' it was powerful stuff and the Pistols were tight and well drilled to cut to the bone, a shock for all the knockers who said they couldn't play" (*Coventry Telegraph* 2013).

After the gig finished, the students' union management refused to pay the band on the basis that songs such The Clash's "White Riot" and the Sex Pistols' "God Save the Queen" (which had an early live airing as "No Future") were fascist anthems. Phil Dunn was president of the Lanchester Students' Union at the time and, in an interview for the *Coventry Telegraph* thirty years later, said: "It was an intense evening all ways round. When the band came on the stage it was pretty electric, with wild pogoing. It felt like the coming of something, like an event. There was a few back-stage dressing room problems, not with damage but lots of empty bottles of Benylin being found afterwards (along with glue, Benylin cough medicine was the cheap and cheerful punk rock stimulant of choice). It was the treasurer who had heard the lyrics and deemed them racist and fascist, and refused to sign the cheques" (*Coventry Telegraph* 2013). Of course, the Pistols and The Clash were far from being either racist or fascist, but this illustrates the way in which the public viewed punk rock at the time. In the end, the student union managers realized that they would have to pay the band and did so.

THE *TODAY* SHOW

Up until late 1976, punk rock remained a cult, with a relatively small following in the United Kingdom. However, an event that took place on television on December 1, 1976, was to change that, and would bring punk to the forefront of the media and into the minds of the general public. This same event also catapulted the Sex Pistols to stardom and fame (or infamy, depending on which way you view it).

UK television in the 1970s was very comfortable. Popular shows included *Coronation Street*, a sitcom set in the North of England that runs to this day; *Opportunity Knocks*, a talent show where hopefuls performed to the public vote; the *Benny Hill Show*, a zany (now seen as very politically incorrect) comedy show; and *Doctor in the House*, a comedy based on the misadventures of the medical personnel at the fictional St. Swithin's Hospital.

Today was a regional news program broadcast at the time by Thames Television, the regional ITV channel serving London. The presenter of *Today* was Bill Grundy. Grundy was born in Manchester in 1923 and began his career as a geologist and part-time journalist and then became a newsreader. He was the first television announcer to present the Beatles on Granada Television (the channel for Manchester) in 1962.

Queen were due to appear on *Today* on December 1, 1976, but canceled their appearance at the last minute, as Freddie Mercury was not well. There was a buzz about punk rock, and the Sex Pistols were quickly lined up as a last-minute replacement. *Today* couldn't have chosen more of an opposite to Freddie Mercury and Queen, whose glam image and multilayered operatic vocals had given them massive stardom in the United Kingdom. Queen were riding on the wave of success after "Bohemian Rhapsody" topped the charts in the previous year, and they were just about to release the *A Day at the Races* album. The Sex Pistols were about to embark on their first major Anarchy in the U.K. tour, and were ready to rise to the challenge and expectation of Grundy and the viewers of shocking punk rockers.

UK television had, and still has, a well-established policy of making nine o'clock at night the pivotal point of the evening's television, a "watershed" before which "all programmes should be suitable for a general audience, including children. The watershed reminds broadcasters that particular care should be taken over inclusion of explicit scenes of sex and violence, and the use of strong language (BBC 2017). The *Today* show was broadcast live and uncensored, and aired at six o'clock in the evenings on weekdays, before the watershed, a time when spoken obscenities were forbidden. Grundy had a reputation for being a penetrating interviewer who wasn't frightened to challenge his guests. He also had a penchant for a drink, and it seemed he may have had one or two before the show. From the outset, it was clear that this program was going to be interesting. The Sex Pistols turned up for the interview in full punk dress, with Johnny Rotten setting out to shock by wearing a swastika armband. They were accompanied by a group of their friends, including Siouxsie Sioux and Steve Severin of Siouxsie and the Banshees. It was clear from the start that Grundy didn't like the young punks, and that he was setting out to show them up on air. His plan to do so, however, backfired badly.

A transcript of some of what happened next is given below:

GRUNDY: They are punk rockers. The new craze, they tell me. Their heroes? Not the nice, clean Rolling Stones . . . you see they are as drunk as I am . . . they are clean by comparison. They're a group called the Sex Pistols, and I am surrounded now by all of them.

JONES [reading from the autocue, ahead of Grundy]: In action!

GRUNDY: Just let us see the Sex Pistols in action. Come on kids.

[A short video of the Sex Pistols playing "Anarchy in the U.K." is shown.]

GRUNDY: I am told that that group have received forty thousand pounds from a record company. Doesn't that seem, er, to be slightly opposed to their antimaterialistic view of life?

MATLOCK: No, the more the merrier.

GRUNDY: Really?

MATLOCK: Oh yeah.

GRUNDY: Well tell me more then.

JONES: We've f°°kin' spent it, ain't we?

GRUNDY: I don't know, have you?

MATLOCK: Yeah, it's all gone.

GRUNDY: Really?

JONES: Down the boozer.

. . . .

GRUNDY Beethoven, Mozart, Bach, and Brahms have all died.

ROTTEN: They're all heroes of ours, ain't they?

GRUNDY: Really . . . what? What were you saying, sir?

ROTTEN: They're *wonderful* people.

GRUNDY: Are they?

ROTTEN: Oh yes! They really turn us on.

JONES: But they're dead!

GRUNDY: Well suppose they turn other people on?

ROTTEN: [Under his breath] That's just their tough s°°t.

GRUNDY: It's what?

ROTTEN: Nothing. A rude word. Next question.

GRUNDY: No, no, what was the rude word?

ROTTEN: S°°t.

GRUNDY: Was it *really*? Good heavens, you frighten me to death.

....

SIOUX: I always wanted to meet you.

GRUNDY: Did you really?

SIOUX: Yeah.

GRUNDY: We'll meet afterwards, shall we?

JONES: You dirty sod. You dirty old man!

GRUNDY: Well keep going, chief, keep going. Go on, you've got another five seconds. Say something outrageous.

JONES: You dirty bastard!

GRUNDY: Go on, again.

JONES: You dirty f**ker!

GRUNDY: What a clever boy!

JONES: What a f**king rotter.

GRUNDY: Well, that's it for tonight. The other rocker Eamonn, and I'm saying nothing else about him, will be back tomorrow. I'll be seeing you soon, I hope I'm not seeing you [the band] again. From me, though, goodnight.

The signature tune played, and the credits rolled. Rotten looked at his watch, Jones started dancing to the music, and Grundy muttered, "Oh s**t!" to himself. The entire exchange was less than three minutes.

THE IMPACT

The impact of the *Today* incident was both powerful and immediate. Julien Temple remembered, "The Pistols had this chance to go on TV and it was just fantastic to be watching it because it just got better and better. It was what they always were, they were a black comedy, a music hall act and the fact that the guy was so drunk was brilliant" (*The Independent* 2006).

Thames TV realized immediately that things had gone very wrong and they went straight into damage-limitation mode. A public apology was given by an announcer and continued to air for the rest of the evening: "Earlier this evening, Thames Television broadcast an interview between Bill Grundy and the Sex Pistols pop group. There was some foul language broadcast which offended many viewers. We very much regret this offensive interview and apologize most sincerely to all our viewers." As Steve Diggle of the Buzzcocks describes it: "It was almost like an atom splitting. The next thing you know some truck driver had kicked his TV in because he was so repulsed. That made it all exciting. That just made legends" (*The Independent* 2006).

Although *Today* was a regional program and seen only by those who lived in and around London, the story hit the national press, particularly the tabloids. The next day the *Daily Mirror* featured the story on its front page with the headline "The Filth and the Fury." Suddenly, punk rock was big news, and everybody had heard about the new music craze and its leading band, the Sex Pistols. The phrase "The Filth and the Fury" would soon be emblazoned across T-shirts and in posters on the bedroom walls of teenagers all over the United Kingdom. It was also later used by director Julien Temple as the title of his Sex Pistols documentary.

In many ways, this event gave us, the young people of the United Kingdom, exactly what we had been waiting for. Here was a group of young punks who just didn't care what they said and who they said it to, and they weren't going to toe the line and accept everything the older generation threw at them.

The word "f°°k" had been uttered on British television on only two previous occasions. The first time was eleven years earlier when critic Kenneth Tynan was asked whether he would allow a play to be staged that featured sexual acts, to which he replied: "Well, I think so, certainly. I doubt if there are any rational people to whom the word 'f°°k' would be particularly diabolical, revolting, or totally forbidden. I think that anything which can be printed or said can also be seen" (Moran 2013). The program resulted in a storm of protest. The second occasion was when Peregrine Worsthorne used the "F" word on the BBC's *Nationwide* program in 1973, which also caused a series of protests.

Bob Geldof of The Boomtown Rats summarized the event in terms of Johnny Rotten: "John was a very smart guy. The catalyst was this very drunk TV presenter. He had been briefed that they were outrageous and how to be outrageous was to say a naughty word on telly" (*The Independent*, 2006).

To the older generation and the public in general, the Pistols had confirmed their very worst fears. These young punks were out to corrupt the youth of the day and wanted to bring down society, and they needed to be stopped at all costs. Before the Grundy incident, punk rock was hardly heard of. The day after the program aired, it became a national phenomenon. The Sex Pistols immediately became outcasts and represented everything that was bad about rock music and youth culture, and council officials up and down the United Kingdom quickly set out to ban the band from playing in their town. Radio stations stopped playing "Anarchy in the U.K." This single incident destroyed the career of Bill Grundy. He was immediately suspended and the *Today* show was soon canceled. He would never work on mainstream television again.

It may be difficult to imagine today just how strong and immediate the impact of this single incident was, and the shock reaction that a few young guys swearing on television could cause. I remember being surprised at the way in which the press picked up the story. According to the *Daily Mirror*, the television switchboard was flooded with calls from angry viewers and the *Mirror* itself received two hundred calls from readers, all of whom were in shock and disgusted by what they had seen on the Grundy show. Famously, one man, James Holmes, was apparently so shocked that he kicked in the screen of his television set. Lorry driver Holmes, who was forty-seven at the time and from Essex, heard the swearing being listened to by his son, Lee, and was so annoyed he took a swing at the TV with his boot. "It blew up and I was knocked backwards he said. . . . I was so angry and disgusted with this filth. I can swear as well as anyone, but I don't want this sort of muck coming into my home at teatime. It's the stupidest thing I have ever done. I dread to think what my wife will do when she finds out." Holmes added, "I am not a violent person, but I would like to have got hold of Grundy. He should be sacked for encouraging this sort of disgusting behaviour." The television station had to admit that "because the programme was live, we could not foresee the language which would be used. We apologise to all viewers." The *Mirror* went on to say that "punk rock groups and their fans despise establishment pop stars and sing songs which preach destruction. They dress as outrageously as possible with the aim of causing maximum shock." The *Mirror* also contained a feature inside the paper under the heading "They're obnoxious, arrogant, outrageous" (Greig et al. 1976).

I went to school that day and everybody was talking about the Sex Pistols and punk rock. I felt quite proud because I was able to say that I had seen the Sex Pistols live a few months earlier, and everyone wanted to know what they were like. Part of me was delighted that punk was now becoming more widely known; another part of me felt sorry that the "secret" was out. I knew that things would never be the same.

EMI REACTION

The Sex Pistols' appearance on *Today* had been arranged by EMI. Of course, they had no idea what was to occur. A team of EMI staff were watching the show and sat in shock as it unfolded. They knew instinctively that they had a big problem. Per McLaren, "I knew the Grundy show was going to create a big scandal. I genuinely believed it would be history in the making and in many regards it was" (McNeil and McCain 1996).

Reaction at EMI was mixed. Senior staff and board members wanted to cancel the Sex Pistols' contract. Many workers in the office and record pressing plant supported the band. The publicity team began to look at ways to maximize the opportunity and publicize the exciting new band that EMI had signed. In the end, the mood returned to damage limitation and protecting their investment. EMI was not about to get rid of the band, at least not yet. That would come a little later.

EMI had an annual general meeting scheduled for December 7, 1976, a few days after the Grundy incident, and quickly crafted and released a press release. They started by setting out the context and explaining the mood of the time: "Today, there is in EMI's experience not only an overwhelming sense of permissiveness—as demonstrated by the content of books, newspapers and magazines, as well as records and film—but also a good deal of questioning by various sections of

Society, both young and old, e.g. What is decent or in good taste compared to the attitudes of, say, 20 or even 30 years ago? It is against this present-day social background that EMI has to make value judgements about the content of records in particular. EMI has on a number of occasions taken steps totally to ban individual records, and similarly to ban record sleeves or posters or other promotional material which it believes would be offensive" (EMI 1976).

The press release then referred directly to the Sex Pistols incident, which "started with a disagreeable interview given by this young group on Thames TV last week, has been followed by a vast amount of newspaper coverage in the last few days. Sex Pistols is a pop group devoted to a new form of music known as 'punk rock.' It was contracted for recording purposes by EMI Records Limited in October 1976—an unknown group offering some promise, in the view of our recording executives, like many other pop groups of different kinds that we have signed. In this context, it must be remembered that the recording industry has signed many pop groups, initially controversial, who have in the fullness of time become wholly acceptable and contributed greatly to the development of modern music." The press release concluded:

> Sex Pistols have acquired a reputation for aggressive behaviour which they have certainly demonstrated in public. There is no excuse for this. Our recording company's experience of working with the group, however, is satisfactory. Sex Pistols is the only "punk rock" group that EMI Records currently has under direct recording contract and whether EMI does in fact release any more of their records will have to be very carefully considered. I need hardly add that we shall do everything we can to restrain their public behaviour, although this is a matter over which we have no real control. Similarly, EMI will review its general guidelines regarding the content of pop records. Who is to decide what is objectionable or unobjectionable to the public at large today? When anyone sits down to consider seriously this problem, it will be found that there are widely differing attitudes between people of all ages and all walks of life as to what can be shown or spoken or sung. (EMI 1976)

DJ Pete Waterman described the event as "the most wonderful coup. You couldn't have bought it. Malcolm McClaren must have thought all his days had come at once" (*The Independent* 2006).

The fallout from the Bill Grundy incident would continue to affect the career of the Sex Pistols for the months to come. The first obvious impact was on their scheduled nationwide UK tour, which is the subject of the next chapter. For EMI, the band's days were numbered, although it was to be another month or so before the label finally realized they had signed an act that they were unable to understand, manage, or cope with.

4

THE ANARCHY IN THE UK TOUR

The Sex Pistols' "Anarchy in the U.K." tour was due to start just a few days after the Bill Grundy incident. The tour had originally intended to showcase the Sex Pistols, with support from The Clash, The Damned, and, from the United States, ex–New York Doll Johnny Thunders and his new band The Heartbreakers. The tour was an ambitious affair, comprising of more than twenty concerts at major venues across the country. It was a big leap from the venues that the band were used to playing; taking the Sex Pistols from small clubs with audiences of 200 or 300 people to theater and concert halls such as Newcastle City Hall, my local venue, which had a capacity of 2,400 to the Glasgow Apollo, which had a capacity of around 4,000.

My friends and I bought our tickets for the Newcastle concert, and I was really looking forward to it. Most of my friends remained loyal to classic rock bands like Led Zeppelin and Black Sabbath, and were not at all convinced about punk music. I managed to convince them to come along to the Sex Pistols concert, but they continued to goad me about my newfound interest in punk rock, and they were certain that the tour would be a commercial failure and that the Sex Pistols would be playing to half-empty halls. I secretly feared that McLaren and the band were moving too fast. "Anarchy in the U.K." was released in November 1976 just before the start of the tour. Reviews of the Pistols' debut single were mixed, and the record was banned from daytime radio after the Bill Grundy incident. BBC Radio 1 John Peel championed the band and continued to play the single, which reached number 38 in the UK charts before being withdrawn by EMI.

John Peel was one of the few UK radio DJs who supported punk, although he never actually managed to witness a full Sex Pistols gig. Peel apparently attended the 100 Club in London on May 11, 1976, during the period that the band had a Thursday night residency at the venue, but he had to leave during their first number to present his show on Radio 1 (John Peel wiki 2017). He also attempted to see them on the Anarchy tour on December 4, 1976, when they were due to play a concert in Derby. Peel drove to Derby from London only to find a handwritten note stuck on the venue door informing fans of the cancellation of the gig. Such was the saga of the tour as councils up and down the country began to cancel concerts and do everything they could to prevent the band from playing in their town.

THE CAST

The Anarchy tour was to be the first major punk concert tour in the UK and featured three of the best new bands alongside the Sex Pistols in the form of The Damned, The Clash, and Johnny Thunders and the Heartbreakers. Malcolm McLaren had originally hoped to feature The Ramones and The Vibrators on the tour, but both these bands pulled out. No matter, the new lineup was strong.

The Damned featured Dave Vanian (David Lett), Captain Sensible (Raymond Burns), Rat Scabies (Chris Millar), and Brian James (Brian Robertson). The Damned played their first show on July 6, 1976, supporting the Sex Pistols at the 100 Club. They also played at the 100 Club Punk Festival on September 20, 1976, and were the first punk group to release a single, "New Rose," which appeared on Stiff Records, on October 22, five weeks before the release of "Anarchy in the U.K." The B-side of "New Rose" was a manic, fast-paced cover of The Beatles' "Help." "New Rose" started with Dave Vanian speaking the lyric "Is she really going out with him?" in homage to the Shangri-Las' 1964 hit "Leader of the Pack."

The Damned's music was fast punk rock. However, their image drew from a variety of popular culture. Dave Vanian was steeped in the legacy of early gothic horror movies. He had been a gravedigger and

changed his name from Letts to Vanian as a play on words of "Transyl-
vanian." He was one of the early influencers of gothic fashion and
would sport black clothing, cloaks, and white face make up, in the style
of Dracula. The *New Musical Express* described Vanian as "a runaway
from the Addams Family" (Tobler 1992). Captain Sensible was the
crazy clown of the band and would dress in outrageous clothes and wear
a red beret. Brian James was the cool leather-jacketed guitar hero, and
Rat Scabies was the typical mad drummer, banging away on his kit.

The Damned mixed goth and rock style with humor, and a Damned
concert was always guaranteed to be an event. Unlike the Pistols, and to
some extent The Clash, The Damned played across the country all the
time. I saw them several times during this period, at concerts in Redcar,
Middlesbrough Rock Garden, and Newcastle Polytechnic. They toured
in October 1976 in support of US proto-punks The Flamin' Groovies.
This was one of their first forays into the provinces, which started to
gain them a new group of fans. The Damned gigged relentlessly, playing concerts at clubs and student unions throughout the country. I
remember a shambolic gig at Newcastle Polytechnic—lots of glasses
flying, much edginess, fights—cutting the set short as a result. We
talked to the Captain (Sensible) in the bar; he held court to a few of us,
telling us how he was an ABBA fan, devouring a packet of crisps, including the packet itself, all in one go. I also remember a gig at Middlesbrough Rock Garden, which finished with an encore of The Captain
coming back on stage stark naked and peeing on the crowd. A Damned
concert was chaos, madness, great fun, and loud, fast punk rock.

The Clash were very different again. Their music started as punk
thrash but soon incorporated elements of reggae and rockabilly. The
Clash consisted of Joe Strummer (John Mellor, lead vocals, rhythm
guitar), Mick Jones (lead guitar, lead vocals), and Paul Simonon (bass
guitar, vocals). The original drummer was Terry Chimes, who left just
before the tour and was briefly replaced by Rob Harper and then by
Nicky "Topper" Headon, who would remain their drummer during
their classic period in the late 1970s. The Clash's lyrics were much
more explicitly political than The Damned and the Sex Pistols and their
rebellious attitude was to have a far-reaching influence that would
stretch further than simply punk rock. Critic Sean Egan summarized
them: "They were a group whose music was . . . special to their audience because that music insisted on addressing the conditions of pover-

ty, petty injustice, and mundane life experienced by the people who bought their records" (Egan 2014, vii).

Strummer had been a member of pub rock band the 101'ers and Jones had been in protopunk band London SS. They were friends of the Sex Pistols and were managed by Bernie Rhodes, an associate of Malcolm McLaren. Jones had seen an early Sex Pistols concert: "You knew straight away that was it, and this was what it was going to be like from now on. It was a new scene, new values—so different from what had happened before. A bit dangerous" (Robb 2006, 151). The Clash made their debut on July 4, 1976, supporting the Sex Pistols at the Black Swan pub in Sheffield. At that time, they featured second guitarist Keith Levene, who met Johnny Rotten for the first time that night and was later to join him in his post-Pistols band Public Image. The next night, members of The Clash and the Sex Pistols attended a concert by New York's leading punk rock band, The Ramones, at London Dingwalls. The Clash then entered a short period of intense rehearsal and played their next gig at a private concert before a small, invitation-only audience in a Camden studio. *Sounds* critic Giovanni Dadamo was in attendance that night and described the band as a "runaway train . . . so powerful, they're the first new group to come along who can really scare the Sex Pistols s**tless" (Strongman 2008, 133). On August 29, 1976, The Clash opened for the Sex Pistols at The Screen on the Green concert. They also performed at the 100 Club Punk Festival, by which time Levene had left the band. The Clash would wear clothes splattered with paint and political slogans. Their early songs include "White Riot," "I'm So Bored with the USA," and "London's Burning," making their political views very clear to everyone.

Johnny Thunders and the Heartbreakers were an American punk band formed in New York in May 1975 from the remnants of the New York Dolls, who had been managed by Malcolm McLaren. Along with Johnny Thunders (John Genzale, vocals, guitar) the Heartbreakers also featured Jerry Nolan (drums), Billy Rath (bass), and Walter Lure (guitar, vocals). Thunders and Nolan had both been members of the New York Dolls. The Heartbreakers arrived in the United Kingdom just as the punk scene was gaining momentum, and developed a following in and around London. Their music was more rock and raunch than thrash, and reminiscent of the Dolls. Johnny Thunders was the archetypical punk rock guitarist. Dolls bass guitarist, Arthur Kane, wrote of

Thunders' guitar sound: "I heard someone playing a guitar riff that I myself didn't know how to play. It was raunchy, nasty, rough, raw, and untamed. I thought it was truly inspired" (Kane 2009 5).

THE FIRST GIG

The four bands set out from London on a tour bus and drove off to play the first concert of the tour. Rather than the expected and highly anticipated tour of major concert halls, what actually followed was a tour of hotel rooms as they traveled from town to town, only to be told that each concert had been canceled, as each local council and promoter buckled to the media and public pressure in order to prevent these nasty punk bands from corrupting the young people of the United Kingdom.

The first three gigs were scheduled for the University of East Anglia Students' Union, Norwich (December 3, 1976), the Kings Hall, Derby (the gig that DJ John Peel turned up to on December 4, 1976), and the City Hall, Newcastle, on December 5, 1976 (the concert that my friends and I had tickets for). All these concerts were canceled. The students at the University of East Anglia held a sit-in protest, to no avail. The Pistols' tour bus headed straight for Derby, where the bands stayed in the Crest Hotel and were met by a group of reporters who would follow them on the tour. It was a cold winter; not the weather to be traveling around the country on a bus. The economic climate also remained poor, with inflation at 16 percent, and the government had just negotiated a £2.3 billion loan from the International Monetary Fund.

In Derby, the local council considered allowing the bands to perform, but only if the Sex Pistols first auditioned for local councillors. The bands refused, although The Damned suggested that they would be willing to do so, which annoyed McLaren and the others. The Damned played one gig and were then sacked from the tour. Newcastle Councillor Arthur Stabler explained that the City Hall gig was canceled "in the interests of protecting the children" (bombedoutpunk website) and so the tour set off for Leeds.

The Sex Pistols finally got to play on December 6, 1976. The concert was at Leeds Polytechnic, where a sell-out crowd gathered to witness the punk package tour, and each band was hungry to perform. Caroline Coon reported on the event in *Melody Maker* (December 11, 1976) and recalls a subdued crowd of students and locals, the majority of whom were new to punk, and would not have seen any of the bands before. The Clash opened the show, with Joe Strummer commenting, "I've been going around for two days thinking Big Brother is really here" (Coon 1976a) referring to the bans that the tour had faced up and down the country. The Heartbreakers and The Damned followed, each band receiving a warm reception. It was the headliners, the Pistols, that everyone was waiting to see, however. Johnny Rotten explained, "We're dedicating this event to local councillors, Bill Grundy, and the Queen." Coon reported: "Unimpressed by the local talents' 'London boys' taunts, he [Rotten] sneers, glares and finally goads the audience into a laughing reaction to his jokes. He steers the band through a trouble-free, thunderously powerful set, but after the encore, even though the students want him back for more, everyone is left wondering what all the fuss is about" (*Melody Maker* 1976). There was much spitting from the crowd as they had clearly been reading how to behave at a punk rock concert. Rotten left the stage covered in gob that night.

David Whittaker was in the audience: "I remember the noise, every band counted each song in and out. This was my first taste of punk. I, like most other people there, just stood and gazed in total confusion, at what was happening on the stage. . . . I saw a guy with green hair, a loud-mouthed Londoner who was there as much to be seen as to see. I also remember Johnny Rotten, in an oversized red waistcoat and oversized, baggy black trousers, aiming negative remarks towards some local Leeds MP who had tried to ban the show" (Whittaker 2008). Johnny Black (1996) recalls Rotten taunting the crowd: "You're not wrecking the place. The News Of The World will be really disappointed. . . . I 'ope you 'ate it! You don't like it, then you know where the exit door is!"

The band was staying at the Draganora Hotel in Leeds, where they were joined by a group of fans. There was an incident in the hotel lobby during which a potted plant was broken, and this was widely reported by the press, who were looking for any opportunity to write about the antics of the punk rockers. Senior staff at EMI were also observing what was happening and were beginning to lose patience with the band.

THE ELECTRIC CIRCUS, MANCHESTER

The Damned had now left the tour and the next concert to take place was at Manchester's Electric Circus on December 9. Local band the Buzzcocks joined the lineup for this gig, replacing The Damned and opening the evening's proceedings. Located just outside central Manchester, The Electric Circus had been a venue for progressive rock and heavy metal bands, but in the mid- to late 1970s it became a venue for punk rock, hosting concerts by all the major bands of the time. As an independent venue that was used to hosting concerts by alternative rock bands, it was one of the few places in the country that would welcome the tour. The gig went well, and as a result, the tour would return to the same venue ten days later. Johnny Black (1996) recalls how the bands were crammed into the Electric Circus' tiny dressing room, waiting for showtime, while outside a group of angry locals chanted: "Get the punks. Kill the bastards." Mounted police and bouncers struggled to admit fans while keeping the violent crowd at bay.

The Sex Pistols had a growing base in Manchester, having played the legendary Free Trade Hall only a few months earlier. The Electric Circus was packed with old and new fans; everyone was eager to see the tour that was making headlines. Paul Morley (2006) reported on the concert and describes The Clash as "London's best rock'n'roll band" and the Sex Pistols as "a band for jumping up and down to. A pop group to the Clash's rock'n'roll and the Heartbreakers' bop rock."

The Pistols' short set on December 9 featured the following songs: "Anarchy in the U.K.," "I Wanna Be Me," "Seventeen," "(I'm Not Your) Steppin' Stone," "Satellite," "Submission," "Substitute," "No Feelings," "Liar," "Pretty Vacant," and "God Save the Queen." The encore was "Problems."

Peter Silverton (1976) reported the gig in *Sounds*, December 18, 1976, and felt that the Pistols got off to a great start: "when Johnny, Glen, Steve and Paul sliced through the crowd (no folding lotus stages for them . . . yet), bounded up the steps and roared straight into 'Anarchy in the U.K.', the kids knew just what to do because they knew the song." However, he also felt that the "band were visibly tired and disorientated by the happenings of the past week, . . . well below maximum power" and that The Clash were probably the best band of the evening.

Pete Shelley remembers the gig fondly: "I thought we played really well. It was the last time we ever played with the Pistols and the last time I saw them play. The Electric Circus had previously been a heavy metal club, but the Anarchy gig turned it round and started punk in Manchester" (Black 1996). Among the audience were members of the Stiff Kittens, soon to become Joy Division, and then New Order. Steven Morrissey, soon to be of The Smiths, was also there, largely to see the Heartbreakers, as he had been a big fan of the New York Dolls and used to run their UK fan club. He wrote a letter about the concert to *Melody Maker* (December 11, 1976): "The likes of the Sex Pistols have yet to prove that they are only worthy of a mention in a publication dealing solely with fashion; and if the music they deliver live is anything to go by, I think that their audacious lyrics and discordant music will not hold their heads above water when their followers tire of torn jumpers and safety pins."

"It was easily the most terrifying concert I've ever been to," remembers Frank Brunger (Black 1996). "There was a violent element in the crowd and the glasses and bottles soon started flying." This was becoming more and more frequent at punk gigs, as local gangs used the concert as an excuse for violence. Peter Hook remembers the second night at the Electric Circus as "just a riot. There were so many football [soccer] fans and lunatics throwing bottles from the top of the flats. It was really heavy, a horrible night. Punk had been completely underground until Grundy. After that, it was completely over the top. There were so many of the punks getting battered" (Lloyd 2016).

THE CASTLE CINEMA, CAERPHILLY

In between the two Electric Circus gigs, the tour rolled into Wales. It was originally planned to call at Cardiff Top Rank ballroom, but when that gig was canceled, a local promoter offered up the possibility of playing at the Castle Cinema in Caerphilly. So, on December 14, the three punk bands rolled into Caerphilly, a small market town in the Welsh valleys. The south Wales people were not ready for punk rock and did their very best to prevent the gig from happening. An outraged resident wrote the following letter to the *South Wales Echo* (1976): "We feel bound to protest against the decision of our local Castle Cinema management to engage a 'punk rock group' already notorious for its dependence on obscenity, blasphemy and open violence."

The gig went ahead and footage of the scene outside the venue can be seen in *The Filth and the Fury* film. It was quite a bizarre, almost surreal situation. A small choir was singing Christmas carols outside in the cold, while a preacher was reading a sermon and trying to convince those entering the venue not to do so. A leaflet was handed out reading: "Even though apparently just a passing fad . . . such trends are clearly part of the fulfilment of Jesus' end" (Sex Pistols Official Website 2018).

The concert was not well attended, with around sixty people in the venue, and it all went off without any trouble. In the audience that night was Steve Strange, who would soon pioneer the new romantic movement and front the band Visage, who had a successful chart with single "Fade to Grey."

The situation continued throughout December. The bands would travel to the next concert, only to find that it was canceled. A gig was scheduled to take place at Liverpool Stadium for December 11 and was hastily rearranged for the famous Cavern Club, where The Beatles started their career. The *Liverpool Echo* of December 7, 1976, reported under the headline "Call for boycott on Sex Pistols":

> An outraged Liverpool councillor today called for a boycott on punk rock group Sex Pistols—who vow to sidestep a ban on their city concert. Councillor Doreen Jones plans to demonstrate outside the club where they hope to play in a bid to dissuade youngsters from seeing the group. "Let's show the rest of the country Liverpool is too good for this sort of rubbish. We don't want them here," she said. The group—who incensed audiences by swearing on the Thames TV program *Today*—heard last night their planned show at Liverpool Stadium had been canceled. A Stadium spokesman said, "The publicity they generate does not persuade me to allow them here. These Sex Pistols advocate Anarchy and we don't want to take the risk." Instead the group hope to stage the concert at a city club. Their manager, Mike [*sic*] McLaren said: "We aren't going to tone down our act one little bit. There won't be any compromises in Liverpool—that's a promise." Asked if this meant the concert would include obscenities, he replied: "Life includes obscenities. Our act reflects life."

However, the concert at the Cavern Club was also canceled and the tour did not get to play in Liverpool.

In addition to the concerts in Leeds, Manchester, and Caerphilly, the tour also managed to play concerts at Cleethorpes Winter Gardens on December 20, and ended with two gigs at Plymouth Woods Centre on December 21 and 22. The first night at Plymouth was well attended; however, the second concert, and the last night of the tour, saw just twenty punters, including six members of the local chapter of the Hell's Angels, turn up to see the bands. Matlock remembers the last gig as "the best of the whole tour, probably because we were all so happy that it was finally over. We didn't even bother to change into our stage clothes, just played for each other" (Lloyd 2016). The tour bus returned to London on Christmas Eve. The Sex Pistols were tired and broke. What had started out as the punk package tour of all time almost ended in disaster.

Toward the end of the Anarchy tour, plans were assembled for the Sex Pistols to play in London, and discussions took place about a possible gig at the Roxy Theatre in Harlesden on December 26 and 27 (not to be confused with the punk club The Roxy, which opened in central London around the same period). Terry Collins, licensee of the Roxy Theatre, told *New Musical Express* (1976: 2) that the Pistols "booked rehearsal time at the Roxy, so I went along to assess them, and I was horrified by their attitude which was absolutely disgusting." Collins also alleged that the band had caused "considerable backstage damage" and that he finally decided not to allow the band to play because he did not "want to condone their attitude." The Roxy Theatre was to host a headline gig by The Clash in 1977.

To most people, the Anarchy tour was a big failure. However, McLaren viewed it in a different light: "We've been banned in virtually every town in the country, they're writing about us all over the world, we make the news at six nearly every night—you can't buy this amount of exposure" (Southall 2007). Indeed, there were those who wondered whether McLaren had engineered some of the bans, including some of the members of the band. He had at the very least played up to the publicity and gone along with some of the exaggerated accounts of the band's outrageous behavior.

PARTING COMPANY WITH EMI

The Sex Pistols were soon gigging again. Malcolm had arranged two concerts in the Netherlands for the new year, one in Rotterdam on January 6, 1977, and another in Amsterdam the following day. They were also booked to appear on the Dutch television show *Disco Circus*. It seemed, however, that the band could not escape the press who were following their every move and were waiting for them at Heathrow Airport as they left for Holland. There was a small incident, which was denied by the band and the EMI representative who was accompanying them. The band were undoubtedly hungover, still recovering from the Christmas and New Year's festivities, and may have been swearing and misbehaving a little. However, the evening news reported that they had "vomited and spat their way" onto the flight under the headline "These revolting VIPs! Sex Pistols in rumpus at airport." *The Guardian* reported that "The Sex Pistols were reported to have abused and spat at passengers and airline officials at Heathrow airport on Tuesday, as they left for Holland. One was said to have vomited" (Knewstub, 2009).

McLaren described the incident: "The KLM situation at the airport was fabricated up to a point. Yeah, the band might have looked a little bit extraordinary; they may have spat at each other. Big deal. And someone may have appeared a little drunk. But they weren't flying the plane, they don't need to be that sober" (McNeill 1977).

Whatever the truth may have been, this was the final straw for EMI, which at this point was looking for an excuse to terminate the Sex Pistols' contract. The corporation had been under pressure internally, from the media, and politically to do something about "this punk band" since the Grundy incident. For example, the conservative member of Parliament for Christchurch and Lymington, Robert Adley, had recently written to the managing director of EMI, Sir John Read, saying, "Surely a group of your size and reputation could forgo the doubtful privilege of sponsoring trash like The Sex Pistols." Bernard Brook-Partridge, who was chair of the Arts Committee and a conservative member of the Greater London Council, went further: "Most of these groups would be vastly improved by sudden death. The worst of the punk rock groups I suppose currently are the Sex Pistols. They are unbelievably nauseating. They are the antithesis of humankind. I would like to see somebody dig a very, very large, exceedingly deep hole and drop the whole bloody lot down it" (Gimarc 2006, 49).

After several internal meetings, during which supporters of the band argued that they should be retained, a decision was finally made to part ways and a statement was issued: "EMI feels it is unable to promote the group's records in view of the adverse publicity generated over the last two months—although recent press reports of their behaviour appear to have been exaggerated." And so, the world's most (in)famous punk group and the world's largest recording company finally parted ways, only three months after they had come together. Asked whether they would consider signing another punk rock group, Sir John Read told the BBC: "Certainly. I am told there is a demand for this style of music and provided we can have groups that don't attract the adverse publicity this group has had; we'll certainly want to be in it."

THE DEPARTURE OF GLEN MATLOCK: SID VICIOUS JOINS THE BAND

The gigs in Holland were to be the last to feature bass player Glen Matlock. Relations between Matlock and the rest of the band had started to become tense during the Anarchy tour, with particular antagonism between him and Rotten. Glen was quieter and more reserved than the rest of the guys. "I think I probably was the most conservative member," reflects Matlock. "But it's all relative. Actually Steve was probably the most out-there guy in terms of hedonistic behaviour and everything. I was more the safe kind of guy; I knew some of what the guys were doing was going too far. We all need a bit of back-up, and I don't think Steve and Paul gave me enough of that in those days, when John was being John" (*Belfast Telegraph* 2013). It also appears that McLaren was manipulating the situation behind the scenes, playing Rotten against Matlock, enjoying the resultant tensions, and believing this situation could play to his advantage through additional friction, incidents, and publicity. John Lydon: "The things I was led to believe about Glen, and I'm sure Glen was led to believe things about me. . . . Somebody told us a f**king crock of s**t and it was nasty, evil, spiteful, vindictive, and manipulative." Matlock: "Malcolm's whole game was to divide and conquer and he did anything he could to perpetrate that" (Black 1996).

Whatever the truth of the matter was, Glen Matlock left the Sex Pistols in February 1977. Reports from the band suggest that he was sacked because he "liked The Beatles" (Dalton 1997) and "he didn't look like a Sex Pistol; he was always washing" (McKenna 2005). Worst still, he was dressing neatly and introducing harmonies to the band's songs. Matlock had provided the musical substance of the band, and without him the Sex Pistols would complete the transition into a loud, crashing, garage-band "wall of sound."

Matlock claims that he left by mutual agreement and later wrote in his autobiography *I Was a Teenage Sex Pistol* (Matlock 2012), that he departed because he was simply "sick of all the bulls**t." On February 28, 1977, McLaren sent a telegram to the *New Musical Express* that officially announced Glen Matlock's departure from the Sex Pistols.

This was undoubtedly a big blow and left the band with a massive problem. Matlock had been the main songwriter and most responsible for all their catchier songs, including "Anarchy in the U.K." and "Pretty Vacant." Matlock soon formed his own band, Rich Kids, featuring Midge Ure (who had been considered for the role of vocalist in the Sex Pistols, and would also feature in Ultravox!, and the massive charity fund-raiser record Band Aid and the global concert that followed, Live Aid), Steve New, and Rusty Egan. Rich Kids set out with a very different image from the Sex Pistols and championed the power pop music genre. Rich Kids blended 1960s pop with punk and had a stylish, "new mod" approach.

Matlock was soon replaced on bass guitar by Johnny Rotten's friend and ultimate Sex Pistols fan Sid Vicious. There was, however, a problem as Sid was not able to play guitar and had to quickly set about learning the instrument. The idea of recruiting Sid was all John's; the other two members thought it was crazy but ultimately went along with it, particularly as Malcolm appeared to approve of the move. Indeed, it is rumored that Sid (real name John Beverley) was the original choice of vocalist, and had been suggested as such by Vivienne Westwood, who had told McLaren to recruit "John" to the band. McLaren had apparently misunderstood his partner and approached John Lydon, rather than his friend John Beverley. Westwood confirms this in her autobiography (Westwood and Kelly 2014): "I was instrumental in Sid being in the Sex Pistols . . . it was me." In some ways, the recruitment of Sid fit well with the punk ethos of the band; after all, punk was all about kids picking up guitars and playing with little experience or initial talent.

Sid Vicious was born John Simon Ritchie on May 10, 1957, in Lewisham, London, to John and Anne Ritchie. Sid's father was apparently a guardsman at Buckingham Palace and a trombone player in a jazz band. Sid's parents divorced shortly after he was born. In 1965, his mother remarried and he took the name of his stepfather and thus became John Beverley. Sid and John Lydon were friends, having met as students at Hackney Technical College. It was Lydon who christened Ritchie "Sid Vicious" reportedly after Lydon's pet hamster Sid, which bit Ritchie. Sid didn't appreciate his new moniker: "I hate the name Sid. It's a right poxy name, it's really vile. I stayed in for about two weeks because everyone kept calling me Sid, but they just wouldn't stop. Rotten started it. He's 'orrible like that, always picking on me" (Dalton 1997).

Sid took to hanging around King's Road and McLaren's shop, SEX. Per Lydon, Sid was "a Bowie fan. He'd do silly things to get his hair to stick up because it never occurred to him to use hairspray. He'd lie upside down with his head in an oven. Sid was such a poseur a clotheshound of the worst kind. . . . He had naivete, which is a good quality, a kind of innocence, but he lost that. He couldn't see dishonesty in people" and he saw "life as a joke" (Dalton 1997).

Sid had been a follower of the Sex Pistols since the start and was in attendance at many of their early gigs in London. There was, however, a darker, violent side to his character, and he was reported as having assaulted *New Musical Express* journalist Nick Kent and was also allegedly responsible for throwing the glass that injured a young woman at the 100 Club Punk Festival in September 1976. Sid was sent to Ashford Remand Centre as a result of the incident. Sid was drummer with Siouxsie and the Banshees for their first appearance at the aforementioned Punk Festival and is also often credited with inventing the traditional punk dance—the pogo.

Sid fit the Sex Pistols completely. While in some respects, John Lydon may have been acting out the part of Johnny Rotten, "John Beverley *became* Sid Vicious" (Dalton 1997). In Sid Vicious, John Beverley found himself, and the Sid persona took over. Sid was pure, authentic punk. He was a raw innocent who threw himself, body and soul, into the Pistols ethos. To many, Sid Vicious would come to represent the Sex Pistols every bit as much as Johnny Rotten.

Almost at the same time as Sid joined the band, another strong character appeared in the Sex Pistols camp. Nancy Spungen became the American girlfriend of Sid shortly after he joined the Sex Pistols. Spungen was raised in Philadelphia and was a disturbed child, being diagnosed with schizophrenia as a teenager. She was intelligent and did well academically, but she had few friends. Nancy was expelled from school at age eleven, and her parents then sent to several other schools. She was a difficult and complex individual who was violent to her sister, allegedly threatened to kill her babysitter with a pair of scissors, and attempted suicide by slitting her wrists. Nancy enrolled at the University of Colorado Boulder when she was 16 but was soon arrested for marijuana possession and then she was expelled after being arrested for storing stolen property in her dorm room. She was soon financing herself by stealing from her family and dealing drugs.

Spungen moved to New York City, where she worked as a stripper and prostitute. She had been hanging around the punk clubs of New York and punk bands the New York Dolls and The Ramones, and as a result, she was known to Johnny Thunders and his Heartbreaker bandmates. Richard Hell of New York punk band Television described Nancy as "a fairly typical suburban girl who worshipped rock stars, she had an exceptionally large drive to be where the action was" and recognized that "she would do absolutely anything to get what she wanted" (Dalton 1997).

In 1976, Nancy moved to London to visit Jerry Nolan of The Heartbreakers, but she had also heard of the Sex Pistols and set her sights on becoming a Sex Pistols lady. The initial target of her affection was Johnny Rotten, who showed no interest in her, so she pursued Sid, and they soon moved in together. It has been said that Nancy introduced Sid to heroin; however, Vivienne Westwood disputes this and points out that he was already using drugs when he joined the Sex Pistols. Westwood claims that Sid said "his mother had given him his first fix when he was fourteen" and that "he was a junkie" (Westwood and Kelly 2014).

A&M

In 1977, McLaren was negotiating a new record deal for the Sex Pistols. There was plenty of interest, with Virgin records and CBS both wanting to sign the band. On March 10, 1977, the Sex Pistols signed to A&M Records. This was another strange choice of label for a punk band. A& M was very much part of the establishment, as had been the case with EMI. A&M Records was formed in 1962 by middle-of-the-road musician Herb Alpert and his partner Jerry Moss. Throughout the 1960s and 1970s, A&M was home to Herb Alpert & the Tijuana Brass, Burt Bacharach, Sérgio Mendes & Brasil '66, and The Carpenters. In the late 1960s, A&M added several British rock artists to its roster, including Cat Stevens, Joe Cocker, Procol Harum, Humble Pie, Fairport Convention, Free, and The Move. However, the Sex Pistols' stay with A&M was short-lived and the label dropped the band within a week.

The signing to A&M was marked by a major press conference held outside Buckingham Palace, the home of the Queen of England. The significance of the palace was clear: this was an opportunity to announce not only the new partnership but also the upcoming release of the Sex Pistols' next single, "God Save the Queen," a new song that had originally been titled "No Future" and had featured in the band's live set during the Anarchy tour. The actual signing had taken place the day before in the A&M offices. After the signing, the band went to SEX to be interviewed and then moved to the Regent Palace Hotel for a press conference. The event can be seen in the Sex Pistols movie *The Great Rock 'n' Roll Swindle*.

The band had been drinking heavily, and after the press conference they made their way to the A&M offices, completely obliterated. Jones and Cook were fighting, Sid Vicious went to the bathroom, where he destroyed a toilet bowl, cutting his foot in the process (there is some disagreement about which happened first) and trailing blood all over the office. While this was all going on, Rotten was swearing loudly at members of the A&M office staff. The next evening, Rotten, Vicious, and their friend and future Lydon bandmate Jah Wobble were drinking in the Speakeasy Club, which was a meeting place for those in the music industry. The Pistols' entourage ran into DJ Bob Harris, who was, at the time, the host of the TV rock show *The Old Grey Whistle Test* (OGWT). Bob Harris was not a fan of punk and had a gentle, hippieish manner, which made him "the enemy." The Pistols approached Harris and his sound engineer George Nicholson and demanded to know why they didn't play the Sex Pistols' music. This soon developed into an argument and a minor scuffle, with Sid allegedly threatening to kill Bob Harris. Harris escaped shaken but unhurt, but his drinking companion George was injured in the brawl, Sid having hit him with a broken bottle. Harris and Nicholson were friends of senior staff at A&M and reported the incident to them.

This was all too much for A&M, and hurried calls were made to Herb Albert, who agreed that the band's contract should be terminated immediately. The A&M record plant was already pressing copies of "God Save the Queen" and nearly all of the twenty-five thousand copies of the single were promptly destroyed. The few that remain in existence are among the most valuable pieces of vinyl in the world, with copies selling at upward of $12,000. The Sex Pistols were without a label again, but they had walked away from the deal with their advance intact.

There were rumors that Yes keyboard wizard Rick Wakeman also had a hand in the firing of the Sex Pistols. This rumor raged in the music press shortly after the Pistols left A&M and claimed that Wakeman had written to A&M urging them to act and terminate the Pistols' contract. The rumors were fueled by the Pistols themselves, with Rotten claiming that both Wakeman and Cockney Rebel frontman Steve Harley had complained about the band. Wakeman and Harley both denied the claim. Rick Wakeman, speaking to *Circus* magazine in 1977, dismissed the allegations:

> That's an absolute load of rubbish. In fact, I'm suing two English newspapers over that because that's really ludicrous. For starters, I've never even heard the Sex Pistols. . . . I'm a born looney, a born idiot sometimes. I was over in Montreux and I read in the papers that A&M had signed the Sex Pistols and to me that band hadn't done anything worse than The Who had done. So I sent a telegram to Derek Green which got incredibly distorted in the press—it was really just a joke telegram. Derek is a really good friend of mine, and I spoke to him on the phone afterwards and we really laughed about it. . . So the next thing that's heard is that the Pistols had left A&M and the label had given no comment. So once again the dear old press got a hold of my telegram to Derek and distorted it beyond all reason. (Farber 1977)

MORE GIGS

The Sex Pistols played their first gig with Sid Vicious on March 21, 1977, in Notre Dame Hall, London, to an invited audience of fifty people. The purpose of the event was to film the band's set for a documentary on punk rock. Sid apparently acquitted himself well, with the Pistols having lost none of their power. At the end of March, the Sex Pistols went to Berlin for a short holiday and were filmed in front of the Berlin Wall; footage of which can be seen in *The Filth and the Fury* movie. It was during this stay in Germany that the band had the idea for a new song, "Holidays in the Sun," which would become their fourth single. Although the band described the city as "raining and depressing," they were also pleased to escape from the madness of London and recent events. Said Rotten: "being in London at the time made us feel like we were trapped in a prison camp environment. There was hatred and constant threat of violence. The best thing we could do was to go set up in a prison camp somewhere else. Berlin and its decadence was a good idea. The song ["Holidays in the Sun"] came about from that. I loved Berlin. I loved the wall and the insanity of the place. The communists looked in on the circus atmosphere of West Berlin, which never went to sleep, and that would be their impression of the West" (Murphy 2002).

Their next gig, on April 3, 1977, was a free, secret show at the Screen on the Green cinema, the scene of a previous Pistols triumph. The audience of 350 first watched a home movie collage of Pistols performances that had been put together by Don Letts and was called *Sex Pistols Number 1*, followed by a short set by girl punk band the Slits. The Pistols played a short set of eleven songs plus two encores and featuring new material, including "EMI" (a song about their short time with the label: "I tell you it was all a frame; they only did it 'cos of fame. Who? E.M.I.") and the single that never was (at least not yet) "God Save the Queen." John Savage (1977b) reported the gig in *Sounds* magazine, writing that the band seemed "frozen in time: Rotten still berates the audience—not quite so wholeheartedly" and that "Vicious stands legs astride, playing adequately, but he *looks* the part." Savage went on, "Rotten is totally mesmeric: the lurker in derelict alleys, a spastic pantomime villain, with evil for real" and felt that "to the audience, musical and stylistic considerations are all but irrelevant" as the Pistols had now become "symbols—us against them—the songs anthems, inviolate from criticism. Just to see them is enough—it's a bonus that they played a good set." Don Letts filmed the concert with his super 8 camera and footage can be seen in Letts' *The Punk Rock Movie.*

During April 1977, the Sex Pistols continued to record tracks for their upcoming debut album at Wessex Sound Studios, London.

5

THE QUEEN'S JUBILEE

God Save the Queen

The year 1977 marked twenty-five years on the throne for Queen Elizabeth II of England. Her Silver Jubilee celebrations took place throughout the country to commemorate the occasion. The actual anniversary of the queen's accession to the throne on February 6, 1952, was observed in church services throughout that month, and the full jubilee celebrations began in earnest during the summer of 1977. The British monarchy remained popular among most of the British population, and many viewed the jubilee as a moment of great civic pride and a brief respite from the economic and social challenges that the country continued to face.

The Silver Jubilee was a big event for the nation. The queen and the Royal Family were held in high regard by most of the public. Shops were filled with memorabilia, such as mugs and plates to "pay tribute for her inestimable services to Great Britain and the Commonwealth" (Hedley 1977). A special emblem was commissioned by King George's Jubilee Trust for use in connection with the Queen's Silver Jubilee Appeal, which was launched by Prince Charles, the Prince of Wales, in April 1977, the proceeds going to new youth enterprises with emphasis on those providing service to the community. School children were given commemorative mugs and coins.

However, against the backdrop of spiraling inflation, many feared that the celebration might be seen as needless and an example of excess and frivolity. Indeed, the palace's plan to introduce a one-off Silver Jubilee Medal was at first blocked by Prime Minister James Callaghan. In the end, however, the argument for celebration won through, as it was felt that it offered a welcome distraction from the social and economic pressures of the time.

In May 1977, the Sex Pistols signed with Virgin Records, the third record label to sign the band in six months. Virgin was eager to have the punk rockers and had been vying for a contract with them. Virgin Records was, in some ways, a maverick record label and shared some of the values of punk rock and the Sex Pistols. The record label was formed in the early 1970s by Richard Branson, who had run a small record shop called Virgin Records and Tapes above a shoe shop on Oxford Street, in the center of London. The shop moved to the Notting Hill section of London in early 1977. Its image was very much of a hippie organization. It sold cheap albums and offered free vegetarian food to customers who would sit on bean bags and listen to the music. After making the shop a success, Branson turned the business into a record label. The name Virgin was, according to Branson (1998), chosen by his colleague Tessa Watts, who suggested "Virgin" because they were all new to business (i.e., "virgins"). The original Virgin logo (known as the "Gemini" or "Twins" logo) was designed by English artist and illustrator Roger Dean, who designed album sleeves for progressive rock bands such as Yes, Uriah Heep, and Magna Carta. The emblem showed a young, naked woman in mirror image with a large long-tailed serpent and the word "Virgin." Virgin's first release, and their biggest success, was in 1973, the progressive rock album *Tubular Bells* by multi-instrumentalist Mike Oldfield.

Branson realized that Virgin had the image of being a "hippie" label and was actively trying to shake that off and expand his roster of artists. He felt that if he could sign some of the new punk bands, he would begin to transform Virgin, and that would be good for business. He had attempted to sign the Sex Pistols on two previous occasions. During the period that the band were with EMI, Branson had asked the label if they wished to release the Sex Pistols from their contract so that they could sign with Virgin. A meeting was organized at the EMI offices, during which Richard Branson met Malcolm McLaren. The two men shook hands and agreed to meet later to seal the deal, the agreement being that McLaren would contact and meet with Branson at a later date. McLaren never did contact Branson, and the opportunity was lost.

Branson sensed that McLaren thought of him as a hippie-turned-businessman, and that he didn't particularly like him. Vivienne Westwood did not share McLaren's dislike of Richard Branson: "Malcolm hated him because they were contemporaries and Branson was already an authority figure. 'Never trust a hippie' Malcolm used to say about Branson. But I liked him" (Westwood and Kelly 2014).

The next opportunity for Virgin to step in and sign the band came when A&M decided to fire the Sex Pistols. Branson immediately contacted A&M and offered to take the band off their hands. "Can I sign them?" he asked (Branson 1998) and the reply was, "If you can cope with them. . . . We certainly can't." Again, the deal didn't happen immediately, but Branson "watched and waited" and shortly afterward the Sex Pistols did indeed join Virgin. Branson felt that by this time Virgin was probably the only major label that could sign them. They were not a large organization of the scale of EMI or A&M, and thus they had no shareholders to protest and no parent company to tell Branson not to do it (Branson 1998).

So, it was on May 12, 1977, that Malcolm McLaren finally went to see Richard Branson. Virgin signed the Sex Pistols for £15,000 for the British rights to their first album, with a further £50,000 payable for the rights for the rest of the world. This money was added to the £50,000 they had received from EMI and £75,000 from A&M. Not bad for a new band of young guys from London and a few months' work.

PUNK GETS ITS OWN LONDON CLUB: THE ROXY

In December 1976, the first club dedicated to punk rock opened in Neal Street WC2, close to London's Covent Garden. The Roxy had been a warehouse for the Covent Garden fruit and vegetable market. In 1970, it was converted to a club called Chaguaramas (after Chaguaramas Bay in Trinidad) by record producer Tony Ashfield, who produced the 1970s reggae star John Holt. It became a gay bar (nicknamed Shageramas) in the mid-1970s. In 1976, the club was taken over by Andrew Czezowski, Susan Carrington, and Barry Jones; the three friends having recognized a real need for a London club dedicated to punk.

Czezowski was managing Generation X, a new band formed by Billy Idol (vocals) and Tony James (bass), who had just left the early punk group Chelsea. Chelsea went on to have a minor hit with their politically themed single "The Right to Work," which tackled issues of unemployment. Billy Idol (William Broad) was a member of the Bromley Contingent and a friend of Siouxsie Sioux. Tony James was originally a member of the seminal and legendary punk band London SS, along with Brian James of The Damned and Mick Jones of The Clash. Generation X were named after a 1960s paperback novel, by Jane Deverson. Generation X played the first concert at The Roxy on December 14, 1976, followed by a gig the next night by Johnny Thunders' band The Heartbreakers. On December 21, Siouxsie and the Banshees played at the club, supported by Generation X. The official opening of The Roxy took place on January 1, 1977, and featured The Clash and The Heartbreakers. It was filmed by Julien Temple, but not screened until 2015 when it was shown on BBC television as *The Clash: New Year's Day '77*.

The Roxy became a very important part of the rise of punk rock in London and gave the genre its own home, a venue where young people could gather and see many of the emerging acts of the time, including, in addition to those bands mentioned above, The Adverts, the Buzzcocks, Wayne County and the Electric Chairs, The Damned, The Jam, The Lurkers, The Only Ones, Penetration, The Police (featuring Sting), Sham 69, Slaughter and the Dogs, the Slits, The Stranglers, Subway Sect, The Vibrators, Cherry Vanilla, Wire, X-Ray Spex, and XTC. The Sex Pistols never played the venue, as the club existed at the time when the band were banned from playing in London—or at least that was the official line. Many believe that Malcolm McLaren wanted to separate his band from the punk scene and keep a level of mystery and exclusivity around the Pistols. It is certainly true that it would not have been difficult for the Sex Pistols to play a secret gig at the club.

The Roxy was a small, dark, sweaty, intimate club compared to the Cavern in Liverpool, where The Beatles started their career. Don Letts became resident DJ and played lots of reggae music for the delighted punters. In 1977, the album *Live at the Roxy WC2* was released on Harvest Records, and featured recordings of performance by Slaughter and the Dogs, The Unwanted, Wire, The Adverts, Johnny Moped, Eater, X-Ray Spex, and the Buzzcocks. The anarcho-punk band Crass would later record the song "Banned from the Roxy," which told the story of how they were not allowed to play at the punk venue: "They said they only wanted well behaved boys, do they think guitars and microphones are just f°°king toys?" The Roxy closed in April 1978 and today is the site of a large store for the swimwear brand Speedo.

GOD SAVE THE QUEEN

Virgin was also ready to release "God Save the Queen." However, staff at the Virgin record pressing plant had other ideas and laid down tools in protest to the song's content. After some discussion, however, production of the new single resumed. The Sex Pistols' second single, "God Save the Queen," was released on May 27, 1977, to coincide with the national jubilee celebrations. The record famously featured a defiant sleeve, designed by Jamie Reid, and was named the greatest record cover of all time by *Q Magazine*, depicting the queen's eyes obscured by the song's title and "Sex Pistols" in the band's trademark cutout letters covering her mouth. Despite its banning, the song reached number 2 on the UK singles chart, with it reportedly being blocked from the number 1 spot for political reasons.

The B side of "God Save the Queen" was "Did You No Wrong," which was one of the Pistols' earliest songs, having been written by founding member, and Swanker, Wally Nightingale and fellow Swanker Steve Jones. The lyrics were rewritten by Johnny Rotten. After being ousted from the Swankers, Wally Nightingale developed an addiction to heroin and was jailed in the early 1980s for drug-related offenses. By 1996, Nightingale was planning a new band called Daylight Robbery. He was also pursuing the Pistols for unpaid royalties of "Did You No Wrong" and was intending to record an album as soon as the money arrived. Nightingale died in May 1996 from drug-related complications; his check from the Sex Pistols arrived the following morning.

Because the Royal Family represented a unifying force that stood above the politics of the time, many took umbrage at the Sex Pistols' defiance. But a good number of British youth saw the jubilee as evidence of their disenfranchisement, and the queen as a symbol of everything that was wrong with their country. McLaren and the Sex Pistols had their own celebratory plans. During the summer months of 1977, the queen embarked on a large-scale tour of the United Kingdom, wishing to mark her jubilee by meeting as many of "her" people as possible. On May 17, her jubilee tour of the United Kingdom and Northern Ireland began in Glasgow and covered thirty-six counties, with greater crowds turning out to welcome the monarch than the city had ever before experienced. The tour continued throughout England and Wales and in Lancashire, in the North West, more than one million people turned out on a single day to the see the queen.

Neil Spencer (2012), writing in the *Guardian*, felt that the Jamie Reid posters were themselves "acts worthy of trial for sedition in some eyes, while in the previous Elizabethan era a character called Johnny Rotten jeering that Queen Bess was 'no human being' would surely have been locked in the Tower." Jamie Reid was beaten up in the street and left with a broken nose and a broken leg that kept him bedridden for two months: "A victim of wearing my own *God Save the Queen* artwork on a T-shirt. I was beaten up outside a rockabilly pub in London" (Back 2002). A Labour MP stated in the *Daily Mirror*: "If Pop music is going to be used to destroy our established institutions, then it ought to be destroyed first" (Back 2002).

SEX PISTOLS NUMBER I

Julien Temple, documentary and music video director, began his career following the Pistols and filming many of their early gigs. Temple was born in Kensington, an exclusive part of London. He went to Cambridge University, where he developed an interest in French film. This, along with his interest in the early punk scene in London in 1976, led to a friendship with the Sex Pistols.

Temple became connected to the Sex Pistols and was fascinated with the whole punk ethos. When interviewed by Lawrence Chua (2000) for *Bomb* magazine at the time of the release of his Pistols documentary *The Filth and the Fury*, Temple said of the Pistols' influence:

> they changed not only my life, but most of the conditions that dictate how you can work and what you can do in the U.K. Without them, the British film industry, which is now mainly driven by young people, wouldn't have happened. . . . The same goes with London fash-

ion. That whole street fashion thing came from the Pistols, really. They changed what was possible to achieve when you were young. . . . the Sex Pistols were always far more to me than a rock band. Nothing since them has been as extremely or powerfully stated. (72)

Temple came across the Sex Pistols by chance. One day, he was walking in the docks area of London and heard the Small Faces song "Whatcha Gonna Do About It" coming from an old warehouse. He walked in and found a new young band "just massacring" the song. He saw guys "silhouetted against this huge window as they were playing, and it was like seeing some weird mutant, insect men from outer space. They had tiny skinny legs, with these huge crepe-soled shoes and black-and-red-striped mohair sweaters on, and this weird cropped, spiky hair." Temple said that he knew at that moment that he "was looking at something truly extraordinary" (Fear 2015). This first meeting had such an impact on Temple that he started attending the Pistols' early gigs and filming what has happening.

Those early films were compiled by Temple as a short twenty-five-minute documentary called *Sex Pistols Number 1*, which took the viewer through the rise of the band during the early period of their career from 1976 to 1977. *Sex Pistols Number 1* is a collage of previously broadcast television interviews and live footage of early Sex Pistols gigs, including footage from the Anarchy tour. *Sex Pistols Number 1* was shown at some gigs, including the Screen on the Green gig, prior to the band taking the stage.

Because of the problem in taking the Sex Pistols on tour, Malcolm McLaren decided to send the film on its own tour of student unions around the country. I remember it screened one lunchtime in a small theater/cinema at Newcastle Polytechnic. The film showed footage of early Pistols gigs; the raw energy and power of the band was incredible. The small cinema was packed and there was a lot of excitement. At the time, this was the closest that many people got to seeing the band. It remains, to this day, one of the best rock movies I have ever seen. After being shown at Newcastle, the file was then sent on to the next student union to be shown. Some of the footage, which seemed awesome at the time, later turned up in Temple's films *The Great Rock 'n' Roll Swindle* and *The Filth and the Fury*.

THE CLASH WHITE RIOT TOUR

While the Pistols were unable to tour or play concerts because of council bans or McLaren's plotting, whichever you choose to believe, other punk bands were out on the road. The Pistols' major competition for the punk crown was The Clash, who during May 1977, toured the United Kingdom on their White Riot tour. White Riot, which was also The Clash's first single, was the first major punk rock tour of the United Kingdom and the first opportunity that fans in the provinces had to experience the new music live. I attended the Newcastle gig, which was the first big punk gig in the city (the Sex Pistols never did play in Newcastle) and it sold out well in advance (Smith 2017). Sadly, most of the tickets had gone to students and not to the working-class kids who The Clash's music was aimed at, which was the source of some aggravation on the night of the gig. When we arrived at the union building for the show, the entrance was surrounded by a group of local punks trying to get in. There were scuffles between the doormen and the punks, who were angry because they couldn't see "their band," who (in their eyes) were playing for a group of middle-class students. This went on throughout the night. Mensi, soon to form the Angelic Upstarts, was present that night (Robb 2006) and would write the song "Student Power" about the chasm between the students and the punks.

There was a great sense of anticipation, edginess, and craziness that night, as was the norm at venues across the country (Green and Barker 1999). Punk was starting to make its mark, but it was still in its early days. We attended the concert because of image, rebellion, and to be part of a new youth culture, as much as for The Clash's music (Sabin 1999). Many were there out of curiosity and because of reports that they had read in *NME* and *Sounds*.

The White Riot tour followed the package tour format (in which several bands toured together, as was very popular in the 1960s) of the Anarchy tour and support came from The Prefects, Subway Sect, and the Slits. The Clash were streets ahead of the support acts (Smith 2017). They looked so different. They wore shirts daubed with political slogans and made "crazy dashes at the audience like a cultural battering ram determined to smash down any faintheart prejudices or lazy preconceptions of what they were about" (Lowry and Myers 2008). The power of their performance and the speed and volume of the music was overwhelming. Their set was short; it was over in what seemed like a few moments. There was lots of pogoing and relentless spitting. Poor Joe Strummer was covered in gob. They looked great, just like their pictures on the cover of the first album. Looking back, it's easy to forget just how new, exciting, and radical punk was. The clothes, the image, the attitude were light years removed from the bands I was into just a few months before.

The White Riot tour was a landmark event in the history of punk and helped establish The Clash as one of the leading punk bands in the United Kingdom. Their accessibility to the fans, in contrast to the distance and secrecy offered by the Pistols, served to help solidify their popularity with punk fans, particularly in the provinces where the Pistols were yet to play many concerts.

THE THAMES RIVER BOAT CRUISE

The climax of the queen's jubilee celebrations came in early June 1977. On the evening of Monday, June 6, the queen lit a bonfire beacon at Windsor, which was followed by the lighting of a chain of beacons across the country. The following day, June 7, large crowds watched the queen drive in a gold coach to St. Paul's Cathedral in London for a Thanksgiving service, which was attended by heads of state from around the world. After the service, the queen and members of the Royal Family attended a lunch at the Guildhall and the queen made a speech to her "subjects": "My Lord Mayor, when I was twenty-one I pledged my life to the service of our people and I asked for God's help to make good that vow."

It is estimated that five hundred million people watched the celebration on television as the procession weaved its way through London and down the Mall, leading to Buckingham Palace, where the queen waved to the cheering crowd from the balcony. This marked the start of street parties across the country. It was reported that in London alone four thousand street parties were held. The final event of the celebrations was a river cruise down the Thames on the June 9, ending with a massive fireworks display.

On the same day, the Sex Pistols took a boat trip down the Thames to have a party to celebrate the release of "God Save the Queen." The boat was named, very appropriately, the *Queen Elizabeth*, and embarked from Charing Cross Pier early in the evening. It was packed, probably to the extent that safety was compromised, with friends of the Sex Pistols (in best jubilee punk regalia), Virgin Records executives and contacts (the ones with long hair and most definitely not in punk regalia), and music journalists. Attendees were provided with a buffet and bar, which, sensing the high probability of drunkenness and trouble, refused to sell any double measures.

The party also featured a short concert by the band. Hungry to play, they delivered an incendiary performance for the small audience, singing "Anarchy in the U.K." as the boat passed the houses of Parliament. The party was raided and ultimately halted by the police, and several people were arrested.

Tony Parsons (writer for *New Musical Express* at the time): "Sid looked fantastic. . . . Malcolm saw the whole thing as performance art, an event . . . there were a lot of hippies on the boat, all these sweet people from Virgin. There wasn't actually a huge divide between hippies and punks back then that we made out there was" (Sweeney 2012).

As the river cruise progressed, a banner, which extended the length of the boat, was unfurled and proudly proclaimed: "New single by the Sex Pistols: God Save The Queen." The plan was for the Pistols to start playing "Anarchy in the U.K." as the boat reached the Houses of Parliament; very appropriate. A police boat trailed the cruisers.

Jon Savage (1977c) reported on the Pistols' performance in *Sounds*: "the band slams into 'Anarchy,' right on cue with the Houses of Parliament. A great moment. It's like they've been uncaged—the frustration in not being able to play bursts into total energy and attack. Rotten's so close all you can see is a snarling mouth and wild eyes, framed by red spikes."

As the band was playing, two police boats pulled up and some policemen boarded the *Queen Elizabeth*. The Sex Pistols continued to play, Rotten screaming out "Problems" directly to the policemen over a wall of crashing sound and squealing feedback. By the time the band reached what was to be their last song, "No Fun," the boat was forced to the dock and everyone was herded off. The event was filmed and can be seen in Julien Temple's Sex Pistols' rockumentary *The Filth and the Fury*. In the film, you can see Richard Branson arguing with the police that the only reason they halted the event was because it was the Sex

Pistols. Most people eventually left; however, Malcolm McLaren refused to do so and can be seen fighting with the police as he left the boat.

Allan Jones (a writer for *Melody Maker* at the time): "Shortly before the Pistols played, police boats started circling us as we approached Parliament. I wouldn't have wanted to be anywhere else at that moment . . . the power was pulled as Rotten was screaming "No Fun" (Sweeney 2012). Several at the Pistols' party were taken to the local police station and duly charged. Malcolm McLaren was charged with causing a breach of the peace, Vivien Westwood was charged with obstructing a police officer, and Jamie Reid was charged with assault. Everyone denied the alleged offenses and was released on bail. The charges were eventually dropped.

VIOLENCE REARS ITS HEAD

Over the next few weeks, violence began to rear its head in London. Several punks were beaten up, including Johnny Rotten and Paul Cook. On June 18, 1977, Johnny Rotten, engineer Bill Price, and producer Chris Thomas were all attacked in London. They were leaving a pub, the Pegasus, in North London during a break from recording when they were attacked by a gang wielding razors. Rotten was taken to a local hospital and received two stitches to a wound in his arm. A few days later, Paul Cook was attacked outside a London tube (subway) station in a similar incident. Cook was attacked by five men with knives and given fifteen stitches to wounds in the back of his head. The Pistols' artist friend Jamie Reid was also attacked by a gang, receiving a broken nose and an injury to his leg. In a second attack later in the month, Johnny Rotten was hurt in Dingwalls nightclub in Camden, London.

It could, of course, be argued that the ethos, music, and lyrics of punk encapsulated, and potentially encouraged, violence. Hoffman (1989) argues that violence is a necessary condition to truly understand and form community, and that it exists everywhere and is around us always. Violence can certainly be found in punk performances, particularly in the early days of the genre. Being present at a punk performance, as a member of the audience, in 1976 and 1977 was to understand, feel, and in many cases, encourage violence. Concerts allowed us to release our frustrations. According to Calef (2009, 151) "good rock is aggressive." He recounts how he once saw "[Small Face] Steve Marriott clobber a security guard in the head with the mic stand because the hapless bloke was trying to stop a fan . . . smoking dope" and how the "applause was deafening."

Calef (2009) also cites The Who and Jimi Hendrix at the Monterey International Pop Festival as examples of how energy and power of violence adds to the intensity of performances. Caroline Coon (1976b) writes of an early Clash gig:

> Three weeks ago at London's ICA, Jane and Shane [MacGowan, later to be of the Pogues], regulars on the new-wave punk rock scene, were sprawled at the edge of the stage. Blood covered Shane's face. Jane, very drunk, had kissed, bitten and, with broken glass, cut him in a calm, but no less macabre, love rite. . . . The Clash were not pleased. "All of you who think violence is tough—why don't you go home and collect stamps? That's much tougher," roared Joe Strummer. Then he slammed into the band's anthem "White Riot."

Punk gigs were often not in themselves encouraging violence. However, perhaps violence was an inevitable consequence of the shock and chaos that ensued. It is argued that some of the most exciting, innovative, and stark changes take place at the "edge of chaos" (Langton 1990).

Spitting at bands was a strange manifestation of punk rock. Spitting is generally considered rude and a social taboo in many parts of the world including the West, while in some other parts of the world it is considered more socially acceptable. Spitting at or on another person, especially onto the face, is a universal sign of anger, hatred, disrespect, and contempt. There remains debate and confusion as to how and when the practice started. Severin of the Banshees states that "it was probably that arsehole Rat Scabies from the Damned" who would spit at the audience, while Johnny Rotten is on record as saying, "I think the audiences gobbing on stage came from me. Because of my sinuses, I do gob a lot on stage, but never out toward the crowd." Julien Temple (the director of the Sex Pistols film *The Great Rock 'n' Roll Swindle*) recalls a Pistols concert: "when Rotten finally came out on stage, it was like Agincourt. There were these massed volleys of gob flying through the air that just hung John like a Medusa" (punk77 2017)

On August 16, 1977, Elvis Presley was found dead on his bathroom floor. With his death, an era came to an end. Presley had become a "grotesque caricature of his sleek, energetic former self. Hugely overweight, his mind dulled by the pharmacopoeia he daily ingested, he was barely able to pull himself through his abbreviated concerts" (Scherman 2006).

SPUNK

Dave Goodman was born in London in 1951 and had played in rhythm and blues and soul bands the Frinton Bassett Blues, the Bluesville Soul Band, and Orange Rainbow during the 1960s. In 1974, he set up his own recording studio, the Four Track Shack, in his parents' garage. Goodman also assembled a large PA system that he rented out. Several bands from the pub rock/punk scene, including Kilburn and the High Roads (featuring Ian Dury) and The Stranglers, rented his PA system.

Goodman first met the Sex Pistols when he rented his PA system to them for an early gig at the Nashville. He was impressed by the Pistols, particularly because they played covers of some of his favorite songs, like The Who's "Substitute," the Small Faces' "Whatcha Gonna Do Bout It," and The Kinks' "I'm Not Like Everybody Else." Goodman built a working relationship with the band and became their sound engineer at all their live shows until mid-1977. He produced the Pistols throughout 1976 and 1977, during which time they recorded early versions of many of the songs that would eventually appear on their debut album, *Never Mind the Bollocks*. Those recordings were released on the unofficial bootleg album *Spunk* during September 1977, prior to the release of their official debut.

A bootleg record is a recording of a session or a performance that is not officially released by a band or artist. It is, in effect, and unofficial and illegal recording. Bootleg tapes were traded and swapped between fans in the 1960s and 1970s. In the late 1960s, bootleg vinyl records made their appearance. The most famous bootleg is Bob Dylan's *Great White Wonder*, released in 1969, which consists of studio outtakes. The bootleg recording was released in a plain white cover and was sold, often under the counter, in small record shops and by mail order throughout the United Kingdom. There was something exciting and illicit about buying bootlegs, which allowed you to listen to recordings of your favorite artists and bands that were not widely available to the public. Another famous bootleg is the Rolling Stones' *Live'r Than You 'll Ever Be*, which originates from an audience recording of a 1969 Stones' concert. In 1975, bootlegs of Led Zeppelin concerts at Earls Court also began to emerge. I recall going to pop festivals in the 1970s and looking for the Bootleg Bus, which was an old ramshackle bus, parked in the field, the seats full of boxes of bootleg records. By the late 1970s, I was searching for bootleg records by the Sex Pistols, including *Spunk*. I remember the excitement of buying a live bootleg of an early Pistols concert, recorded at Nottingham Boat Club in 1976. The quality was terrible, as the recording had obviously been made on a cheap tape recorder to the extent that the music slowed down toward the end of the record as the batteries in the tape recorder began to fail. Nonetheless, it offered a rare opportunity for me to listen to the Sex Pistols live, raw, in concert. I never did manage to buy a copy of *Spunk* at the time.

Many believe that *Spunk* is superior in sound and energy to *Never Mind the Bollocks*. The album certainly captures the raw, live sound of the Pistols in full flight. There was some suspicion at the time that Malcolm McLaren was secretly behind the release of *Spunk* in breach of the band's contract with Virgin. McLaren denied responsibility for *Spunk*, but he also admitted that he preferred it to *Never Mind the Bollocks* (Clinton 2003). The album features Glen Matlock on bass, while *Never Mind the Bollocks* features Steve Jones and Sid Vicious (who was learning the instrument at the same time as the recording sessions). *Spunk* was eventually given an official release in 1996 by Virgin Records as part of a limited-edition double-CD reissue of *Never Mind the Bollocks*.

Several songs on *Spunk* were listed with early formative or simply incorrect, titles including "Lazy Sod" ("Seventeen"), "Feelings" ("No Feelings"), "Just Me" ("I Wanna Be Me"), "Nookie" ("Anarchy in the U.K."), "No Future" ("God Save the Queen"), "Lots of Fun" ("Pretty Vacant"), "Who Was It?" ("EMI"), and "New York (Looking for a Kiss)" ("New York").

To many people, *Spunk* is the definitive Sex Pistols album. For example, on September 1, 2008, Allan Burridge wrote in a review on *Amazon*:

If you're after THE album to own as a classic either of The Pistol's themselves, or punk music as an era in our rock history, then look no further than this. Down here in what many would regard as "sleepy old Dorset," we were as on the ball in 1977 as the rest of the UK with this album. Word went around about the bootleg record stall at Wimborne Market having copies of *Spunk*, so nipping out from work 5 minutes early one lunch hour on market day to get one was the order of the day . . . it was going for a fiver, but the stall-holder at the market sold his for a tenner, and with the buzz going around about it, it was the "must-have" LP of the day and if he'd asked fifteen you'd have paid it. It was THE vinyl album to own and have as part of your collection, and when you hear it you will understand the reasons why. It blows the *Never Mind The Bollocks* album right out of the water, The Pistols were wired to the effing mains when they re-corded these far superior and crunchy versions of the tracks you have come to know and love.

So, for many of us, *Spunk* give us a sneak preview of the album that was soon to follow.

"Pretty Vacant" was released on Virgin Records as the Sex Pistols' next single at the beginning of July 1977, and a promotional video for the record was shown on *Top of the Pops*. The single gave the band their third hit and rose to number 7 in the UK singles chart. "Pretty Vacant" is arguably the band's most commercial and catchy song, and was written by bass player Glen Matlock.

The Sex Pistols were keen to get out on the road again, but the possibility of bans remained, so Malcolm and the guys decided guerrilla tactics were called for. This fit well with the concept of the band and the Situationist movement on which they were based, so in August a secret tour of small venues was arranged, preceded by a tour of Scandi-navia. The UK tour was known as SPOTS (Sex Pistols On Tour Secret-ly) and is discussed in the next chapter.

6

SPOTS (SEX PISTOLS ON TOUR SECRETLY)

August 1977

The Silver Jubilee celebrations were over and all was not happy in Britain. A few days after the celebrations, eleven thousand pickets and protesters clashed with police in West London in support of a strike at a photo-processing plant. The leader of the miners' union, Arthur Scargill, brought a bus full of miners from the North of England to London to show solidarity and join the protest. On the opposite side, a right-wing organization, the National Association for Freedom, organized deliveries to the plant to try and break the strike. Other far-right organizations were also growing and gaining support in a country that was far from content. The National Front was causing tensions and young black people and the police were clashing in major cities, particularly in London. The scene and mood in the United Kingdom was quickly moving from one of celebration to one of discontent. An extreme example of this was seen in Northern Ireland, where in some areas the queen was greeted by the people as "The Queen of Death."

It would be easy and somewhat convenient to portray the punk movement as a direct result of the discontent in the country, and to some extent that would be true. However, the punk movement was not yet a massive and strong call to arms of the youth en masse. Mick Hume (2012), in his essay "It's Not 1977 All Over Again," lays the start of the punk scene as an "elitist posture of a style-conscious few against the

mainstream rather than a mass youth movement." Hume believes that it
was the outrage of the mainstream media and the aftermath of the Bill
Grundy incident that caused punk to come to life. Hume goes on to
state that once the media turned punk into a national phenomenon, it
captured the imagination of the bored generation, desperate for change
and wanting something to happen that they could "own." They saw
punk as a "reaction against both the abysmal music clogging the charts
of the mid-Seventies and a national culture that appeared stuck in the
past." Siouxsie Sioux said, "We hated old people, always going on about
the war: 'Hitler, we showed him!'" (Hume 2012).

Over the August bank holiday weekend, more than fifty arrests were
made because of street battles during the Notting Hill carnival. In football (soccer) grounds across the country and farther afield, organized
hooliganism was ruining the experience for many. Manchester United
was banned from the UEFA (Union of European Football Associations)
Cup after fans rioted during a game in France. For most music fans,
things continued as it if nothing was happening, and bland adult-oriented rock remained popular. The best-selling albums in the United Kingdom were *Arrival* by ABBA, Fleetwood Mac's *Rumours*, *The Sound of
Bread*, and the Eagles' *Hotel California*. In the United States, Robert
Stigwood and the Bee Gees were working on *Saturday Night Fever*
with disco music at its height. Elvis Presley died and seventy-five thousand fans lined the streets of Memphis for his funeral. The Ramones
were gaining fans, having released their second album, *Leave Home*,
earlier in the year. In the United Kingdom, punk bands were forming
across the country and The Clash, The Damned, The Stranglers, and
The Vibrators all released debut albums.

SCANDINAVIAN TOUR

In July 1977, the Sex Pistols were booked to play a tour of Scandinavia.
Just before the tour was due to start Sid Vicious' girlfriend, Nancy
Spungen, appeared in court for carrying a truncheon in her handbag.
Nancy said that the truncheon was for her own protection. The court
threatened to send her home to the United States, but she was saved
when Sid revealed plans to marry her.

When the Pistols arrived at Heathrow Airport to fly to Copenhagen, Denmark, Sid realized that he had forgotten his passport and had to return to his flat to find it and catch a later flight. The press were, as usual, waiting at the airport hoping to get a story. The *Daily Mirror* (1977) reported that the band threatened photographers and threw chairs around the airport. The band was not accompanied by their manager, Malcolm McLaren, because he was in Los Angeles working on the new Sex Pistols film with director Russ Meyer.

The dates of the 1977 Scandinavian tour were:

July 3 and 14: Daddy's Dance Hall, Copenhagen, Denmark
July 15: Beach Disco, Diskotek Ostra Stranden, Halmstad, Sweden
July 16: Mogambo Disco, Helsingborg, Sweden
July 17: Discotheque 42, Jonkoping, Sweden
July 19: Club Zebra, Kristinehamn, Sweden
July 20: Pinvinen Restaurant, Oslo, Norway
July 21: Studenter Samfundet, Trodheim, Norway
July 23 and 24July 24: Barbarellas Disco, Vaxjo, Sweden
July 27 and 28: Happy House, Student Karen, Stockholm, Sweden

Songs performed during the tour included "Anarchy in the U.K.," "I Wanna Be Me," "Seventeen," "New York," "Satellite," "No Feelings," "Holidays in the Sun," "Problems," "Pretty Vacant," "God Save the Queen," and "No Fun."

During the tour, Sid formed a relationship with a young girl named Teddie Dahlin. Teddie was sixteen years old and the translator for the Norwegian leg of the tour. Teddie found the Pistols to be "different . . . to anyone else I knew. They all had short hair. John Lydon and the sleeping guy [Sid] had theirs standing on end, which looked very strange and outlandish. . . . John's was dyed quite red and it made him look scary and strangely insane" (Dahlin 2012). Teddie and Sid soon struck up a friendship, which developed into a short romance that continued for the remainder of the tour.

Teddie recalls being shocked at the level of spitting by the audience during the concerts: "the crowd had started to chant 'spit, spit, spit!' John and Sid spat in the audience. What they hadn't anticipated was that the audience would spit back. . . . I thought it was disgusting. . . . John had to stop the music and appeal to the audience to stop spitting or else they would leave the stage" (Dahlin 2012). Sid introduced himself to Teddie as John, explaining that he only recently had taken that name and "kept forgetting he was Sid." She found Sid to be a "sweet guy" and felt that they both "sensed that our time together would be short" (Dahlin 2012).

Giovanni Dadamo reviewed the Stockholm concerts for *Sounds* and reported:

> New boy Sid still seems a bit uncomfortable onstage but his playing's by no means incompetent. Paul Cook was reliably solid as always with the foundations, Steve Jones had his share of fine moments and Rotten is simply more compelling, authoritative and unique than ever. . . . And "No Fun" really was quite superb, including that chilling moment when Rotten's voice becomes a low mean growl that's so close to Iggy the hairs on the back of the neck stand on end. Like a spiritualist medium for a few seconds, speaking in another's voice. But then it's Rotten again, that distinctive Holloway taunter back in the driver's seat. (Dadamo 1977)

Johnny Rotten chose to wear a tuxedo for the concert and Dadamo felt that it made him "look more like one of those lethal ventriloquist's dummies that come to life and bite people's necks in old horror movies (*Dead of Night*, for example) than ever." He also described Rotten's "awkward yet artful rubber-limbed actions" as a "what's the marionette operated by someone who's having an epileptic fit" (Dadamo 1977).

THE START OF THE SPOTS TOUR

Banned from playing and unable to tour openly, in the summer of 1977 the Pistols played a series of secret club dates. The "SPOTS" Tour (Sex Pistols On Tour Secretly) visited Wolverhampton Lafayette (the Pistols were advertised as "SPOTS"), Doncaster Outlook ("Tax Exiles"), Scarborough Penthouse ("Special Guests"), Middlesbrough Rock Garden ("Acne Rebel"), Plymouth Woods ("The Hamsters"), and Penzance Winter Gardens ("Mystery Band of International Repute"). The gigs all took place over the last week of August and the first week of September 1977. This period is sometimes termed the "Summer of Hate," in direct contrast to 1967's "Summer of Love," and reflected the violent mood of the time. In the United States, several young girls died at the hands of the Los Angeles "Hillside Strangler," and in New York the "Son of Sam" was stalking and killing young women.

For the first night of the tour, the Sex Pistols traveled to the Midlands for a concert at the Lafayette Club in Wolverhampton. The gig was attended by "Peter Don't Care" (punk77 2017), who reported that the gig was "uncomfortably packed" with "even queues for the toilets of this small club, what held about 400–500 tops. And it was ten deep at both upstairs and downstairs bars. Everyone seemed to have had the same idea, stock up now while you can before 'they' come on. Cos no-one wanted to miss the notorious freak show when it hits town! There were all walks of life in here tonight . . . the fans, the curious and the twisted all wanting a glimpse of something extraordinary." The band arrived onstage late, finally appearing at midnight and walking on completely unannounced. Peter reported how the "crowd went wild as Johnny sneered 'Hello Wolverhampton.'" They started the set with "God Save the Queen" and "there was pandemonium everywhere rebounding all around the club and the seething masses were swaying like a football crowd." You can feel the excitement of seeing the Pistols in Peter's account:

> You could see the glassiness in Johnny's laser beam eye and seeing the Pistols in the flesh lived up to the what I had expected and more. . . . Johnny Rotten an arm's length away scrutinises the crowd with a demented stare as he informs us there is "no future, no future for you!" He is decked out with a smattering of talcum powder rubbed into his dirty yellow spiky barnet and covering the shoulders of his black suit jacket. . . . His baggy blue tartan bondage strides were rounded off with a pair of the brightest red brothel creepers you've ever seen. It took a few seconds before the shellshock opening had sunk in. You've got to remember this was the real thing! The band we had read about, heard about this was the Pistols!!! (punk77 2017)

Nancy Spungen attended the gig, or as Peter wrote, "Sid's bird the 'Nauseating Nancy' was standing at the back of the stage leaning against the back wall next to the little door that leads to the tiny dressing room. She was drinking, smoking and chewing gum, watching Sid all the time with her arms folded" (punk77 2017).

The gig was a big success and a great opening to the tour. The Sex Pistols were clearly excited and pleased to be back playing on stage in England, their home, and the crowd couldn't believe their luck in seeing the band. The audience ceremoniously covered the band in beer, spit, and other missiles, and Peter summarized the collective feeling as: "This is the real thing! To see them perform no more than 3ft away [which is still something I will never get over] is something else, larger than life. Whatever you read about em in the papers they were so much better and probably worse!" (punk77 2017).

A new song, "Belsen Was a Gas," was premiered that night with the controversial lyrics focusing on the famous concentration camp. Johnny Rotten announced the song as their new single, which may have been intended at the time, but in the end never took place. As often, there were hints of violence that night, with glasses being thrown at the band, the Pistols "trod a very dangerous path" and "caused some wild reactions everywhere they went." This gig was no exception and the Lafayette Club was "full of nutters and a nasty place to be." The set was completed with an explosive rendition of "Pretty Vacant" and Peter slowly "stagger[ed] out the club in the pissing rain" knowing that he was just "present at something special" and that he had just "witnessed a musical phenomenon" and the "best 60 minutes I will probably have in my entire life" (punk77 2017).

The second night of the tour called at the Outlook Club in Doncaster, which is now long gone, buried under a large interchange. For this concert, the band was billed as The Tax Exiles. Reviewer Pete Scott remembered the gig for the violence of the doormen. He wrote: "One thing I really didn't like were the scenes which went down prior to the set, when the bouncers threw their weight around with great impartiality." And Rotten berated the crowd, too, describing them as "the worst audience I've ever played to" (Scott 2015).

SCARBOROUGH PENTHOUSE, AUGUST 24, 1977

When there were whispers that the Pistols might be playing some secret dates, I was determined to see them. I picked up on hints of gigs through the press and the radio; there was no internet in those days. I also rang around local venues and managed to find out the location of most of the secret gigs. The most local gig for me was Middlesbrough Rock Garden, a venue that I often visited for punk gigs. But sadly, I had a dilemma: I had tickets for the Reading Festival that weekend, and the festival started on the Friday night, which was the night of the Rock Garden gig. And to complicate matters further, I had a carload of mates who I had promised to take to the Reading Festival. I decided that the best solution was to go and see the Pistols on Thursday in Scarborough, drive home that night, and then get up the next morning and drive to Reading with my mates. And that's exactly what I did.

I rang Scarborough Penthouse, the gentlemen answering the phone would only tell me that a "Special Guest Band" would be appearing on Thursday night. They wouldn't be drawn as to whether it was the Pistols, and when I asked the guy directly I was told that I would just have to come along and find out. But it seemed pretty obvious that the Pistols were going to play Scarborough. I figured that there might a lot of demand, and the venue wasn't selling any advance tickets. So the only thing to do was to make sure we arrived early. So, on Thursday morning, my girlfriend, a mate, and I set off for the seaside, and sunny Scarborough. We arrived around lunchtime and found the Penthouse. There were a few punks hanging around, but no line had formed yet. We went to find a chip shop and passed the Pistols walking down the street, which confirmed to us that the gig was indeed taking place.

A few others arrived, so we formed a line and waited. We must have stood for five or six hours until the Penthouse opened its doors, by which time the line was right down the street. The Penthouse Club was a small venue, in an upstairs room as I remember, and could only have held a few hundred people at the most. The stage was set up with large crowd barriers in front of it to make it pretty impossible to climb on stage. The room soon filled up, and by the time the Pistols took to the stage it was absolutely rammed. The atmosphere was electric and the Pistols were incredible. Sid was new to the band and just learning to play bass, but he looked great, just the part. John was amazing, sneering and snarling, hanging off his mic stand, and at times covered in spit from the crowd. Steve Jones was the ultimate rock guitar hero, all swagger in his leather jeans, and Paul Cook was smashing away at his drums. And they were LOUD and fast.

The set was quite short; they were on stage for less than an hour. They started with "Anarchy" and played most of the yet-to-be-released

Never Mind the Bollocks album. The set list was something like "Anarchy in the U.K.," "I Wanna Be Me," "Seventeen," "New York," "EMI," "Holidays in the Sun," "No Feelings," "Problems," "Pretty Vacant," and "God Save the Queen." They definitely finished with "No Fun." We braved it in the scrum down in front for some of the set, but I eventually bottled it and took up a vantage point at the back, standing on a chair. Too much spitting and pogoing down the front for my liking. My mate tried to tell some punks to stop spitting at John, but they took no notice. The stairs were lined by the local police as we left; they were presumably expecting trouble, but there wasn't any. Everyone started singing "Pretty Vacant" right into the faces of the policemen as we left. Luckily, the police took it all in good spirits.

We drove back home, getting back in the early hours of the morning. I had a few hours' sleep, and then I got up, picked up my mates and drove down to Reading where the festival was headlined by Golden Earring, Thin Lizzy, and Alex Harvey. Not much punk on show that year (although Wayne County and Ultravox! played), but there was lots and lots of mud. Another mate went to see the Pistols at the Middlesbrough Rock Garden and said they were awesome. That gig at Scarborough in 1977 was the last time I saw the Pistols until a reunion show at Brixton in 2007, but the Scarborough gig still sticks in my mind as a very special event. At the time, there really was no other live band like the Pistols. The songs, the image, the energy, the volume, the secrecy of the event—all made their gigs like no other.

MIDDLESBROUGH ROCK GARDEN, AUGUST 25, 1977

The following account of the Middlesbrough gig was told to me by Bill Gillum (personal communication 2017):

> The Sex Pistols seemed to be getting banned from playing anywhere in 1977, I seem to recall. So, when I heard that a band called Acne Rebel were playing at Middlesbrough Rock Garden I thought it could be the Pistols playing under that name to get a gig. My thoughts were that Sid Vicious had acne and he was a rebel, which were clues to who was playing. I rang up the Rock Garden and the girl on the other end of the phone was vague when I was asking if the Pistols had been booked. There was a fair bit noise behind her as she

was speaking and I appealed to her by saying "I would make the journey from Sunderland to Middlesbrough by bus if it wasn't the Sex Pistols playing. She hummed and hawed and then believe it or not the noise turned into a band playing "Pretty Vacant!" I shouted down the phone so she could hear me "that's the Sex Pistols playing!" It was unmistakably Johnny Rotten on vocals. The girl on the phone eventually admitted that it was the Pistols so I reserved two tickets for me and my girlfriend to go to the show that evening.

When we got there the atmosphere was buzzing with excitement and a feeling of trouble and violence in the air. I couldn't believe it. We two were dressed in our "denim suits" and everyone else it seemed was dressed in bin liners, with millions of safety pins and chains. To say we felt out of place was an understatement, but at least I had spiky hair in keeping with a lot of the crowd.

I suddenly realized that I had been little doubt of a few pounds as I paid at the door, so I spoke to one of the bouncers and was drawn to see the manager. I knocked on the manager's door and it opened to what seemed like a meeting of the Kray twins firm! The manager didn't look too happy at my request but said "giving this change" and I was glad to leave in one piece and with my money!

The gig itself was short, lasting maybe only thirty minutes with one encore. I have never seen a better gig before or after this one. The atmosphere, sheer charisma, menace, and excitement, it had everything. Johnny Rotten in particular was totally charismatic; his beady eyes constantly scanning the audience. To give John credit, from start to finish he was spit and gobbed on. He took it all in his stride; people were filling their mouths with beer and spitting it out all over the band, who just kept playing on. The ring of bouncers around the stage and started punching those members of the crowd who was spitting at the Pistols. I remember Sid Vicious had bare arms, cut numerous times and bleeding, a result of (I assume) some serious self-harming. The gig, and the entire band, were totally electrifying. This gig has stood out for me as been a truly one-off experience that could never be repeated. Sheer magic!

The Sex Pistols were interviewed after the gig at the Rock Garden, Middlesbrough. The text below is reproduced from a transcript on Les Dementlieu Punk Bibliotheque (2017) website. Larry Ottoway interviewed the band for local radio station Radio Tees. The interview gives an insight into the band's mood at the time.

LARRY: Right Johnny, fantastic thing tonight, what did you think of it?

JOHNNY ROTTEN: I didn't.

L: You thought what?

JR: I did it, I didn't think about it, I just did it.

L: You just did it eh, what do you think about M'boro? (At this point, a girl kisses Johnny.)

JR: Well don't swallow me for f**ks sake!

L: I'll have a word with someone else, right, we'll go back to Johnny Rotten. What do you think of M'boro, The Rock Garden, fantastic, eh!

JR: It's not bad for a laugh.

L: Is it the best place you've been yet?

JR: NO!

L: Which is the best?

JR: I dunno, I can't remember, Wolverhampton.

L: Wolverhampton, what's wrong with the Rock Garden then?

JR: Nothing at all.

L: But it's good, innit. What's it feel like being a sort of bogey man to everyone in Britain over the age of 20?

JR: I don't give a s**t.

L: You don't give a s**t.

JR: Why should I, we outnumber them.

. . . The interview continues . . .

L: I gather Malcolm's been over in America, negotiating film rights.

PK: How do you know?

L: I read about that in one of those crap magazines.

VOICE: Well don't believe the crap magazines then.

L: That's wrong, is it?

JR: He wasn't negotiating film rights, he was just getting someone to make the bloody thing.

L: And who's gonna make it.

JR: Russ Meyer, we think. We don't wanna do it.

L: What sort of film that's gonna be then?

VOICE: Sex film.

JR: Awful, terrible, hideous.

ANALYSIS OF THE SPOTS CONCERTS

The SPOTS tour saw the Sex Pistols playing at their very best. The band was hungry to play to a home crowd and the fans had waited a long time to see their heroes perform. The reviews of these concerts on this short tour were unanimously positive. Julien Temple felt that the Pistols were "more than a band" and talked of their "theatrical presence onstage" (Lydon and Zimmerman 1995). He continued: "When I saw them play . . . it was an earthquake in the first stages."

But there was much more to a punk performance in 1977. Double (2007) argues that punk draws from popular theater forms such as music hall and stand-up comedy and that the way they use "costume, staging, personae, characterization, and audience–performer relationships" is as important as the music. The SPOTS tour was an important milestone; the band was finally out there reclaiming their crown as the kings of punk. How much the band was real and how much manufactured by both the media and McLaren is arguable. Similarly, how much McLaren had designed the concept of the Pistols and how much occurred by chance remains open to debate. McLaren is quoted as seeing the band as "my Sex Pistols: sexy, young, subversive and stylish boys" and argues that he was using them to "help me plot the downfall of this tired and fake culture" (McLaren 2007). Smiths' front man Morrissey (2013) would later declare "their riches" as "overwhelming" and felt that they were "not the saviours of culture, but the destruction of it." Licht (2005) saw the Pistols as "manufactured by McLaren as a kind of art project." Webb and Lynch (2010) characterize the Pistols as "nihilistic, negative, destructive, ambivalent, chaotic." That wasn't the Pistols which I experienced. I felt uplifted, positive, and refocused during and after the performance (Smith 2015).

The purpose of the Sex Pistols' tours of the country are also open to debate. It has been said (Bromberg 1989) that, in the case of early forays into the North of England, McLaren "sent the Sex Pistols packing on a road trip through the North with [road manager] Nils Stevenson . . . while he began shopping the new tape to record companies." In the case of the SPOTS tour, Bromberg (1989) believes that "McLaren found [roadie] Boogie's idea of sending the group out on the road to outlying provincial towns . . . oddly appealing . . . got the Sex Pistols out of McLaren's own hair by appearing to give in to Rotten's complaints that they had been kept off the road for too long." To Rotten and the rest of the band, the opportunity to play outside of London represented freedom. In the case of early gigs, this was freedom from McLaren and his hangers-on. In the case of the SPOTS tour, it was a freedom to simply play, to show that they could play, and for Rotten to show that he was in charge of their future and not McLaren.

The McLaren strategy was apparently one of "deliberately avoiding not only advance publicity but also all venues in any of rock's most widely accepted centres" (Kent 1977). This can be seen as an early example of "guerrilla gigs." Indeed, *Melody Maker* (1977) announced:

> the Sex Pistols, for many months' musical outcasts in their own country, are about to set out on a guerrilla tour of Britain. . . . With the band arriving unannounced at a venue, leaving only a few hours for word to spread on the local grapevine. If word gets out before the day of the concert and the details are published, the concert will be scrapped. The band have been deliberately booked into low-key ve-

nues, mainly independent clubs off the big circuits. The aim is that word-of-mouth will avoid the vast crowds and possible trouble that advance publicity would bring.

Che Guevara saw the guerrilla fighter as a social reformer who fights to "change the social system." In a similar way, the Pistols were using rock performance to threaten the status quo. You can perhaps draw parallels between the guerrilla nature of these gigs and approaches to guerrilla warfare (Smith 2015), and the Maoist Theory of People's War, which divides warfare into three phases (Tse-Tung and Zedong 1961). Phase one involves earning support through propaganda (i.e., via the music press) and attack to the status quo. In phase two, initial attacks (gigs) are launched. The forays into the provinces would characterise this phase. In phase three, conventional warfare (the concert tour) is used. The SPOTS tour, and earlier attempts to tour such as the 1976 Anarchy tour, where most gigs were canceled because of bans, would characterize this final phase. Smith (2015) presents an analysis of one of the gigs on the SPOTS tour in the following table.

Table 6.1.   Table 6.1 Analysis of SPOTS Concerts.

DIMENSION	NOTES OF ANALYSIS
The Performer: The Sex Pistols	The Pistols were hungry to play. They hadn't been able to in the UK for some time because of concert hall and council bans, or so it seemed. They felt that Malcolm was preventing them from playing. They wanted to show that they could perform (Lydon and Zimmerman 1995), and they now had a full set of songs. Sid was new and needed to play with the band. He was bare chested, his skin covered in scratches and the blood of self-mutilation. They were dressed as punk heroes, and appeared as a confident, accomplished rock band.
The Performance	A loud, straightforward rock set. Much more professional, confident, and polished than the first time I saw them. The set consisted of songs from *Never Mind the Bollocks*. This was a crazy, manic rock spectacle, and so different from the performance I had experienced in 1976. This was a band at the top of their game; they knew it, and so did we.
The "Puppeteer": Malcolm McLaren	McLaren was already planning his next step: a movie based on the story of the Sex Pistols. Sending the band out on tour gave him a chance to work on the movie. McLaren almost certainly planned the secret nature of the tour as another way of creating chaos and publicity.
The Audience	Everyone was there to see the Pistols and had lined up for hours in order to be able to do so. Some were dressed as

	punks, many had long hair. Some were fans; some were there out of curiosity. Everyone went crazy. Lots of spitting at the band.
Place	A seaside town in Yorkshire. A small club venue that regularly hosted rock bands. The Pistols performance caused quite a stir in the town, and there was a heavy police presence. The threat to the status quo was spilling out of the club onto the streets.
Context	Punk was now in full swing. The majority of the population was shocked by it and performances of the notorious Sex Pistols. Punk was becoming mainstream and would soon implode as the Pistols did a few months later.
Me	I was exhilarated by the Pistols' performance and the simple fact that I was seeing them again. I was surprised by how good they were, and how much they had become a traditional rock band. I was overwhelmed by the event and the illicit excitement of seeing something that was banned and viewed as rebellious and shocking.

After the tour, Sid Vicious found himself a new flat in Maida Vale. He signed up for a seven-year lease, which would run until 1984. Malcolm McLaren said at the time, "That's okay. He'll be dead by then" (Wood 1988).

At the beginning of September, former Pistols bass player Glen Matlock launched his new band The Rich Kids.

7

NEVER MIND THE BOLLOCKS, HERE'S THE SEX PISTOLS

Autumn 1977

The Sex Pistols debut album, *Never Mind the Bollocks, Here's the Sex Pistols*, was released on October 27, 1977. Its release was preceded by the singles "Pretty Vacant" (July 1977), which describes perfectly the teenage apathy of the time, and "Holidays in the Sun" (October 1977), the lyrics of which are based on the Pistols' trip to Berlin and the growth in low-cost package holidays at that time.

THE SINGLES

"Pretty Vacant" is arguably the band's most commercial, poppy single and is written by bass player Glen Matlock. According to Matlock, the song's main riff is based on the tune of "S.O.S." by ABBA. The song reached number 6 in the UK singles chart and resulted in the band's first appearance on the main British chart music TV program *Top of the Pops*. The appearance was actually a video of the band that was taped at ITN Studios in London. The Pistols were tossed out of the studio for throwing cans of lager at the cameraman and had to return the next year to complete the video shoot. The B side of "Pretty Vacant" is a cover of Iggy Pop and the Stooges' song "No Fun," which was a favorite of the band and had been included in their live sets for some time, often played as the encore. The *New Musical Express* made "Pretty Vacant" single of the year in 1977.

"Holidays in the Sun" was the Sex Pistols fourth and last single. It was released on October 14, 1977, two weeks before the release of *Never Mind the Bollocks*. It reached number 8 in the UK singles chart. The song was inspired by a short holiday that the band took in Jersey, one of the Channel Islands that lies between England and France. This was followed by a trip to Berlin. Johnny Rotten said, "We tried our holiday in the sun on the Isle of Jersey, and that didn't work. They threw us out" (Sex Pistols Official Website 2017). Whether they were actually thrown out is unclear. Rotten went on to say: "Being in London at the time made us feel like we were trapped in a prison camp environment. There was hatred and constant threat of violence. The best thing we could do was to go set up in a prison camp somewhere else. Berlin and its decadence was a good idea. The song came about from that. I loved Berlin. I loved the wall and the insanity of the place. The communists looked in on the circus atmosphere of West Berlin, which never went to sleep, and that would be their impression of the West. I loved it" (Sex Pistols Official Website 2017). Steve Jones said, "'Holiday in the Sun' was inspired by our trip to Berlin, by the wall, where it was raining and depressing. We had to escape from London at the time, the song pretty well sums up the trip" (Murphy 2002).

It is often said that the opening riff of the song is similar to that of The Jam's first single "In the City." Lead singer of The Jam, Paul Weller, confirmed that he had a fight with Sid Vicious in London's Speakeasy Club over the issue: "He started it and I finished it. I don't know if anyone can claim any victory. He just came up to me and he was going on about 'Holidays in the Sun' where they'd nicked the riff from 'In the City.' I didn't mind them nicking it—you've got to get your ideas from somewhere, haven't you? Anyway, he just came up and nutted me. So I returned it'" (*Uncut* 2017). The B side of the single was "Satellite," one of the band's early songs about some of their initial performances in the satellite towns around London.

The impact of the first four Sex Pistols singles cannot be underestimated. "Anarchy in the U.K." was the initial call to arms for punks throughout the UK and still sends shivers down your spine when it is played today. "God Save the Queen" was the perfect remedy for the Queen's Silver Jubilee celebrations, causing excitement and controversy. "Pretty Vacant" was the perfect punk pop song, and "Holidays in the Sun," with its crashing chords and sneering vocals from Rotten, completed a quartet of rock 'n' roll singles never to be equaled.

NEVER MIND THE BOLLOCKS, HERE'S THE SEX PISTOLS

Never Mind the Bollocks, Here's the Sex Pistols is one of the most important rock albums of all time, fusing classic slamming rock chords with sneering, searing vocals and lyrics. The song titles, in their own simplistic school-boy humor, portray the story of the Pistols and perfectly capture the feelings of the youth of the time. In 1987, *Rolling Stone* magazine named *Never Mind the Bollocks* the second-best album of the previous twenty years. In 1993, writers of the *New Musical Express* voted it the third-greatest album of all time. In twelve short songs on a perfect piece of black vinyl, the Sex Pistols simply, and seemingly effortlessly, blew away everything that came before them and set the bar for anyone who dared to follow. "EMI" tells of their short period at the label, "New York" sarcastically portrays the US punk scene, and "Seventeen" and "Problems" discuss the frustration and social isolation of 1970s teenagers.

The album was controversial in several ways; many people found the word "Bollocks" offensive, with several record stores refusing to carry it and some record charts refusing to list the album, displaying simply a blank space in its place. The original title of the album was *God Save Sex Pistols*, but this was changed on the suggestion of Steve Jones (Strongman 2008), who said he had picked up the phrase from some fans. It is, in fact, a working-class expression for "stop talking rubbish."

The album cover was designed by Jamie Reid, who presented the title and the characteristic Sex Pistols logo against a DayGlo yellow background. The cover was voted the best album cover of the 1970s (Superseventies 2017): "It wasn't the pop phenomenon that interested me," says Reid. "I saw punk as part of an art movement that's gone over the last hundred years, with roots in Russian agitprop, surrealism, dada and situationism. . . . The publicity generated by the Pistols' antics made it unnecessary to put their faces on records." "They were ugly anyway," Reid once said. The *Never Mind the Bollocks, Here's the Sex Pistols* cover flaunts what he calls "cheap hype." He had to revise his design continually because of changes in the album's title and contents. "It caused me enormous aggravation," says Reid. The ransom-note lettering was quickly imitated by hundreds of punk bands.

Recording of the album started in March 1977 at Wessex Sound Studios with producer Chris Thomas and engineer Bill Price. Sid Vicious was new to the band and still learning to play his bass guitar, so Malcolm McLaren convinced previous bassist Glen Matlock to play on the sessions. Matlock agreed at first, but because of a disagreement over payment, he ultimately declined and did not play on the album. Instead, guitarist Steve Jones played the bass tracks as well as his own lead guitar. Vicious played on one song, the new track "Bodies." During the recording of the album, the Sex Pistols changed labels from A&M to Virgin, yet recording continued. There was a lot of discussion about the track list; the initial plan was not to include any of the band's singles; however, in the end, all singles were included. A Virgin spokesman states, "We've put the singles on the LP because most people wanted it that way" (Heylin 2000).

Before the official release of *Never Mind the Bollocks, Here's the Sex Pistols*, two other Sex Pistols albums were released in competition with the official LP. In October, the *Spunk* bootleg was released featuring high-quality recordings of demos of the songs, recorded at an earlier session with Dave Goodman as producer. *Spunk* is often considered to be of superior quality, with versions of the songs that matched the live quality of the band's performances. A French pressing of the album on Barclay Records was due for release one week before the official Virgin album. As a result of this, Richard Branson rushed production of *Never Mind the Bollocks, Here's the Sex Pistols* in order to release it one week earlier than planned.

Despite being banned by many major retailers, *Never Mind the Bollocks, Here's the Sex Pistols* debuted at number 1 in the UK album charts, having had advance orders of 125,000. It continued to sell well through independent record shops.

THE SONGS

There was a lot of discussion in the press as to the appropriateness of including the band's singles on the album. However, on reflection they fit well with the remainder of the Pistols' repertoire and their inclusion meant that the album formed a complete collection of their works.

The album opened with the band's fourth and final single, "Holidays in the Sun." "Holidays in the Sun," although not their strongest single by any means, is an excellent opener with its crashing chords setting the scene and pace for what was to come. Indeed, Steve Jones' guitar work on the song was rated number 43 in *Rolling Stone's* 100 Greatest Guitar Songs of All Time.

"Bodies" was a new song and quite controversial. It's about abortion and the lyrics contain a lot of swearing and some graphic descriptions of the terminated fetus. It is the only song on the album on which Sid Vicious plays bass. It is also the fastest and heaviest track and often quoted as an influence on hardcore and thrash metal. The song is about a fan named Pauline from Birmingham who had been in a mental institution. Legend has it that she stalked the band in their early days. According to the lyrics, she carried her dead fetus in a bag on her side. Johnny Rotten, when asked if the song is anti-abortion, is quoted as saying: "No. Quite the opposite. No, no. Early on I had an acceptance of what life really is. We lived in two rooms and we had an outdoor toilet. My mum had a miscarriage. And this isn't against my mum, but— this could have been a brother or a sister for me to play with and I had to flush it down the toilet. I mean, that strikes you. And that's like an abortion. I'm not anti- or pro-abortion. Every woman should have the choice when they face it. But that was a grim Steptoe & Son world. My mum was heartbroken. And if you construe that as being anti-abortion, then you're a silly . . . sausage" (Odell, 2005). "Bodies" was often played as part of the Pistols' set in their later days.

"No Feelings" is about a narcissistic character with no feelings for anyone else except himself. John Lydon said in an interview, "The song is from the idea of someone being completely selfish, which I'm not. I like to imagine being in that frame of mind. I'm insulting myself really. That happens a lot" (Rachel 2014). The song is very wordy, which makes it a challenge to perform live. Lydon explains, "Some of the songs I've written have so many words it's almost unbearable. 'No Feel-ings,' for instance: I think it's 16 to 18 lines where I don't take a breath. Now, live, that's tempting fate. But I managed to do it. I found the knack. I love pushing those boundaries. You can't cut up a verse like that because it would become out of context. It's the monologue that's necessary to paint the proper picture of someone in a state of babbling confusion" (Rachel 2014).

"Liar" is generally believed to be about Malcolm McLaren. Rotten and McLaren had a volatile love/hate relationship and Rotten often believed Malcolm to be a manipulative liar. After the death of Malcolm McLaren, Lydon was asked if he missed McLaren. Lydon responded, "Malcolm McClaren didn't inspire. He took credit for things he didn't do. So f**k him. I'm not great at dealing with death, I have to say" (Nissim 2010).

"God Save the Queen," an iconic piece of rock 'n' roll, still stands as one of the greatest rock singles of all time. *Rolling Stone* includes it in the list of five hundred greatest songs of all time, and the Rock & Roll Hall of Fame lists it as one of the five hundred songs that shaped rock 'n' roll. *Sounds* magazine made it single of the year in 1977. In 2002, *Q* magazine ranked it number one in its list of the 50 Most Exciting Tunes Ever. According to Glen Matlock, his base line was inspired by The Move's 1960s smash "Fire Brigade." Drummer Paul Cook denies that the song was created specifically for the Silver Jubilee, stating "it wasn't written specifically for the Queen's Jubilee. We weren't aware of it at the time. It wasn't a contrived effort to go out and shock everyone" (Lydon and Zimmerman 1995). The phrase "no future," which runs through the song, became entwined with punk rock. On reflection, *Never Mind the Bollocks, Here's the Sex Pistols* would not have been complete without this song. "God Save the Queen" would continue to make an impact for many years to come. In 2010, it was ranked among the ten most controversial songs of all time in a poll conducted by the Performing Right Society for Music. It was re-released in 2012 to coincide with the thirty-fifth anniversary of its original release and the Queen's Diamond Jubilee. Speaking on BBC News at the time, John Lydon made it clear that he was not happy with this release, saying, "I would like to very strongly distance myself from the recent stories and campaign to push 'God Save the Queen' for the number one spot. This campaign totally undermines what the Sex Pistols stood for. It is certainly not my personal plan or aim. I am proud of what the Sex Pistols achieved and always will be but this campaign totally undermines what the Sex Pistols stood for. This is not my campaign. I am pleased that the Sex Pistols recordings are being put out there for a new generation, however, I wish for no part in the circus that is being built up around it." The song was covered by many artists, including Motorhead, Anthrax, and (in live performance) the Foo Fighters.

"Problems" sums up the nihilistic attitude of the Pistols. Rotten spits out the lyrics and concludes that "the problem is You!" This was a live favorite, with Rotten staring at the crowd and screaming, "The problem is You!" at those fans at the front.

Side two of the album opens with the song "Seventeen." "Seventeen" is one of the Pistols' earliest songs, was originally titled "I'm a Lazy Sod," and featured in their live sets from the very early days. The lyrics are very antihippie and portray punks as lazy and not caring about their future.

"Anarchy in the U.K."—what more can be said about this song? It's the track that started it all for the Pistols and put a marker down as to their stance and intentions. It still sends shivers down the spine today, and reverberates even forty years later.

> Forty years ago today, one of the most iconic singles in the history of punk music was released and the Sex Pistols were launched on a trajectory towards equal measures of fame and notoriety. Anarchy in the UK may have only edged into the Top 40, reaching the not-so-heady heights of 38, but its cultural impact still reverberates. It was the musical detonation of frustration at the status quo. It wasn't the articulation of a manifesto for a new economics but a wrecking ball of a song that these musicians aimed straight at the establishment. (Williamson 2016)

Malcolm McLaren asked Rotten and Matlock to write a song about submission; he was thinking in terms of bondage and sadomasochism. John and Glen had other ideas, however, and thought Malcolm's original concept was sleazy. So, they decided, as a joke, to write a song about a submarine mission. Hence, "Submission."

The opening riff of "Pretty Vacant" is immediately identifiable. It's a great pop/rock song. I can still remember the impact the band's performance on *Top of the Pops* had on me. Rotten spat out the word "vacant" taking great pleasure in emphasizing the last syllable to make it sound like the word "c**t." The song was covered by Joan Jett and Black Grape, and Joey Ramone covered the opening riff as part of his cover of "What a Wonderful World." Noel Gallagher of Oasis chose "Pretty Vacant" as one of his song choices for Desert Island Discs on BBC Radio 4.

"New York" is another song that was written by Rotten as a joke about Malcolm; in this case, specifically about how he admired the New York scene and the New York Dolls in particular. Paul Cook states, 'New York' was originally Steve's riff, and John came up with the lyrics to wind up Malcolm. There's still a lot of talk that New York started the punk scene and we ripped them off. People think we were influenced by it. We weren't. The track was ultimately a put-down of that scene" (Here's the Artwork 2017).

The album closes with "EMI," a "tart rejoinder to their former record company" (Rock Portraits 2017). Somehow, what should sound petty instead turns grandiose. "The material is glorious. It's one of my fave of the lot," insists Rotten. The song (and the album) ends with the words, "Hello EMI / Goodbye! . . . A & M," and then a raspberry is blown. The perfect closing track to the perfect debut rock album.

CRITICAL RECEPTION

The album was unanimously well-received by critics and fans alike. It was recognized as a landmark LP, not just for punk but for rock 'n' roll. Initial reviews were extremely positive.

Kris Needs (1977) reviewed the album for *Zigzag* magazine at the time and said,

> The title says it all really. Ignore the press hysteria, dopey articles in *Rolling Stone* and cross-country panic/fear/loathing over "those foul-mouthed Sex Pistols". This album transcends it all . . . and also puts paid to the ignorant bastards who still say the Pistols can't play or are morons. Even those who know the songs from gigs'll be surprised at the sheer attack and overwhelming density of the soundunlike a lot of groups the Pistols and producers Bill Price and Chris Thomas have got a killer sound right first time . . . but then I s'pose the songs have had time to mature and they weren't too proud to spend a bit of time in the studio to get it right. The result is a raging Berlin Wall of gut-wrenching power chords from Steve Jones, Paul Cook's simple and just right powerhouse drumming and the metronomic roar of Sid's bass. [Note the comment about Sid's bass playing, although he

did not actually play on the album, a fact which Needs probably could not be aware of at the time.] It's all topped with John's phenomenal voice, which can slide from spine-chilling no-feelings coldness to frenzied manic wailing. He packs the maximum punch and effect into every syllable he delivers. . . . Yes, this is a direct, honest, no bulls°°t album which contains some of the most vital rock songs of this decade, brutal, real and full of energy and passion. Let's face it. This album would be a monster even if it was mediocre, bad even. . . . Never mind cos it's a stunner. Even better than the build-up built-up. Never mind the bollocks here's the Sex Pistols."

Jon Savage, reviewing the album in *Sounds* magazine at the time said, "It's very powerful. It's a very good rock 'n' roll album. It excites me. I want to dance. So will you. It's authentic. . . . As rock 'n' roll, can't be faulted . . . . Still. Feel somehow that new songs smack of a creeping contrivance . . . and, yeah, what's fine on a single as blast wears me down with nihilism over an album. Believing in nothing, on plastic at least, makes you unassailable, but leaves a funny taste" (Savage 1977a)

Billboard magazine (1977), reviewing the album on its release, declared it "loud, raucous and irreverent, this LP delivers as promised. This is punk rock at its best, with no let-up. Once it begins there's no getting up for air until the record ends. It's all simple riffs and elemental chords with a machine gun beat, but nobody does it better. Included here are all the notorious hits that so shocked the English establishment. Once you get past the rawness of it all, it becomes apparent that this band can craft some very relevant tunes."

Never Mind the Bollocks, Here's the Sex Pistols was eagerly awaited by the band's growing fan base, which included punks and a more general rock audience, all of whom were keen to hear the band on vinyl. It must be remembered that, apart from the singles, the rest of the album had not been heard by the fans other than the small number who were lucky enough to see the Pistols play live. Advance orders of 125,000 resulted in the LP debuting at number 1 in the UK album charts the week after its release on October 28, 1977. I remember the excitement of going to a record shop that day to buy the album. Many of the main outlets refused to stock the LP, so I had to go to a relatively small record outlet at the bottom of town to buy my copy. I went home on the bus proudly holding my copy of the album in its garish sleeve, hoping people would notice me and what I was carrying, which I felt made an important statement at the time.

THE LEGACY

Never Mind the Bollocks, Here's the Sex Pistols is generally recognized as one of the most important rock albums of all time. It is certainly considered one of the best albums, if not the best, of the punk genre. In 1993, the *New Musical Express* voted the album the third-greatest of all time. In 1987, *Rolling Stone* magazine voted it the second-best album of the previous twenty years, behind only the Beatles' iconic and ground-breaking masterpiece *Sgt. Pepper's Lonely Hearts Club Band*.

In 2013, when interviewed for the BBC television program *When Albums Ruled the World*, Noel Gallagher of Oasis said of the album's opening with "Holidays in the Sun": "As soon at that starts, everything that has gone on before is now deemed f**king irrelevant, as soon as he [John Lydon] starts anti singing." He then said of "Pretty Vacant," "One of the 1st things you learn when you pick up the electric guitar is that riff." He then further commented, "I made 10 albums and in my mind they don't match up to that, and I'm an arrogant bastard. I'd give them all up to have written that, I truly would."

The *Zagat Survey Music Guide* (2003) said of the LP: "Be afraid, be very afraid . . . from the harsh reality of the lyrics to the throbbing melodies spit from the guitar, this historically significant, quintessential punk album—loud, snotty and angry youthful anarchy in all its glory—defined a new genre of music and culture and instantly made many popular bands obsolete. With hard-rock production that other bands would kill for, radical Johnny Rotten and the lads created a phenomenon that lives up to the hype."

In *VH1's 100 Greatest Albums*,

> An amazing record, *Never Mind the Bollocks* collects the handful of great Sex Pistols singles, recorded on the fly amid U.K. tabloid vilification and a self-created air of apocalyptic meltdown. The great songs on the album—none more than a few minutes long and built from the bricks of the most rudimentary riffs—are twisted psychodramas that rush headlong into the frontier of working-class young-man rage with an intensity that no other band could capture. Johnny

Rotten's lyrics—direct, blunt, biting—were like antisocial haikus that shone the spotlight of Rotten's scorn out, out, out, accusing, denouncing. It also sounded great. The production was minimal, the playing was primitive, the result was impossibly catchy and exciting. The Sex Pistols were great, then gone. At least they were spared the indignity of trying to follow up on the perfection of their debut. And, for enough cash, they will still come and play the old songs. It has become their final revenge. (Hoye 2003)

In *1,000 Recordings to Hear Before You Die*:

Never Mind the Bollocks doesn't really need any hype. Its snarled refrains and bellicose chants—"No future for you!" Rotten sneers throughout "God Save the Queen"—signal that this is a profoundly different rock and roll enterprise. The song writing's minimal. There's, like, zero finesse in the playing. And yet when the band lunges into "Pretty Vacant" or "Anarchy in the U.K.," it unleashes an undeniable force, leading to explosions of awesome magnitude that proved key to the then-developing ethos of punk. Fans loved the Sex Pistols because the band's music mirrored and magnified the decay they saw all around them. People who loathed the band considered its music (and its tactics) fresh evidence of Society's decline. Both sides, at least, agreed on the existence of a downward spiral. (Moon 2008)

RICHARD BRANSON AND THE OBSCENITY CASE

The album was subject to a wave of censorship from the media and record stores throughout the United Kingdom. In London, the police visited all the shops owned by Virgin Records warning them that they faced prosecution under the 1899 Indecent Advertisements Act for displaying posters of the album cover in their windows. The shops had to either remove the displays or cover the word "Bollocks" on the record cover. The front cover of the *London Evening Standard's* November 9, 1977, issue announced that "Police Move in on Punk Disc Shops," reporting that a Virgin store manager in Nottingham had been arrested for displaying the cover of the record in the window of his shop. It seemed that Richard Branson had asked the manager, Chris Seale, to do so in order to test the system and that "it would appear" that he had "willingly set himself up as a target." Policewoman Julie Dawn Storey saw the record display in the shop window and informed Chris Seale that she believed the word "Bollocks" contravened the law and that he may be liable for prosecution. The shop was then visited by the police on three further occasions, each time being warned to remove the album. Each time, they did as the police suggested but then immediately put it back in the window display as soon as the police left. As soon as Chris Seale was arrested, Richard Branson declared that he would cover all of the manager's legal costs and help him to fight the case. Branson hired the high-profile Queen's Counsel John Mortimer to defend the case.

The case was well publicized in the national press and was heard at Nottingham Magistrates Court on November 24, 1977. During the hearing, John Mortimer pointed out that national newspapers, including the *Evening Standard* and *The Guardian*, had both included the album's full title *Never Mind the Bollocks, Here's the Sex Pistols*, and that they had not been prosecuted. Mortimer pointed out that this was thus a clear case of discrimination. He also suggested that the word "Bollocks" was only considered to be obscene because it appeared on the cover of punk rock album by a controversial band such as the Sex Pistols. Mortimer then went on to produce expert witnesses who successfully demonstrated that the word "Bollocks" was not in fact obscene and was a well-known old English term used to refer to a priest and, in the context of the title, simply meant "nonsense." The outcome of the case was thus: "Much as my colleagues and I wholeheartedly deplore the vulgar exploitation of the worst instincts of human nature for the purchases of commercial profits by both you and your company, we must reluctantly find you not guilty of each of the four charges" (Patterson 2007).

The story was to return to the headlines in 2017 when a group of young ladies traveling on a Jet2 flight were thrown off the plane for wearing T-shirts with the "offensive" slogan "bitches on tour." The girls were on their way to Majorca for a hen party. Richard Branson offered the group free flights to Las Vegas and a three-night stay at the Tropicana hotel. Branson said he was shocked that the group were ejected from the flight, and that their story reminded him of the 1977 obscenity case when a Virgin employee was arrested over the title of the Sex Pistols single "Never Mind The B******s." Sir Richard said, "Never mind the b******s, it's their hen-do. When we released The Sex Pistols classic record, we were arrested over its colourful title. We want to help these ladies 40 years on enjoy their hen-do after they were kicked off their flight over a word on their T-shirts. Virgin Holidays has been welcoming hen parties since 1985 and we hope all 18 of these ladies have a brilliant time painting the town red in one of my favourite cities" (Griffiths 2017).

CHART IMPACT

Never Mind the Bollocks, Here's the Sex Pistols debuted at number 1 on the UK album charts in November 1977. However, the rest of the charts did not reflect what some were declaring "the year of punk." Number 2 in the charts was occupied by *The Sound of Bread*, number 3 by *40 Golden Greats* by Cliff Richard, and number 4 by *20 Golden Greats* by Diana Ross and the Supremes. The rest of the top 10 featured Genesis, David Bowie, Leo Sayer, Fleetwood Mac, and Santana. The only other punk/new wave album was *No More Heroes* by the Stranglers.

The Sex Pistols' debut album was released in November 1977 on Warner Brothers Records in the United States. Its impact there was minimal, reaching number 106 in the Billboard charts. In 1977 and 1978, the US charts were dominated by Fleetwood Mac's *Rumours* album and the Bee Gees' *Saturday Night Fever*. This was still very much the years of adult-oriented rock and disco. Even American new wave was having little commercial impact on the mainstream charts. The Ramones' third and most successful album, *Rocket to Russia*, reached number 49 in the US Billboard album chart. Popular films of the time were *Star Wars*, *Rocky*, *Saturday Night Fever*, and *Close Encounters of the Third Kind*. Popular music stars were Rod Stewart, the Eagles, the Bee Gees, Barbra Streisand, Fleetwood Mac, Paul McCartney and Wings, and Hot Chocolate.

So, new wave and punk were making inroads in the United Kingdom and the United States, but the mainstream music scene remained one of pop, traditional rock, and upcoming disco as characterized by the Bee Gees and the craze around the *Saturday Night Fever* movie. The biggest impact of punk was by the Pistols themselves in the United

Kingdom with the massive success of *Never Mind the Bollocks, Here's the Sex Pistols.*

HAPPENINGS IN THE UNITED KINGDOM AND THE UNITED STATES

Autumn of 1977 in the United Kingdom remained one of unrest and change. In September, glam rock star Marc Bolan of the band T Rex was killed in a car crash, just two weeks before his thirtieth birthday. His girlfriend, Gloria Jones, was driving the car and was seriously injured in the accident. Also in September, English FA Cup holder, Manchester United, was expelled from the European Cup Winner's Cup after their fans rioted in France. They were later reinstated on appeal. In October, undertakers went on strike in London, leaving more than eight hundred corpses unburied. This was also the period of the reign of terror of the Yorkshire Ripper. On October 10, missing twenty-year-old prostitute Jean Jordan was found dead near Manchester, and later in the month police in Yorkshire appealed for help in finding the Yorkshire Ripper, who was believed to be responsible for a series of murders and attacks on prostitutes across the north of the United Kingdom for the past two years prior. Rock band Queen dominated the music scene, releasing their power ballad "We Are the Champions" and their album *News of the World* in the same month. On October 27, former Liberal Party leader Jeremy Thorpe denied allegations of the attempted murder of Norman Scott, a male model with whom he was also accused of having a homosexual relationship. In November 1977, firefighters went on their first ever national strike in support of a large 30 percent wage increase. Later in the month, the first major hypermarket was opened in Washington, Tyne & Wear, in the North East of England. On November 22, British Airways inaugurated regular flights to New York City from London via the supersonic Concorde. On December 14, another prostitute, this time a twenty-five-year-old woman from Leeds, Marilyn Moore, was injured in an attack believed to have been committed by the Yorkshire Ripper. On December 21, four children died at a house fire in the West Midlands as Green Goddess fire engines (an outdated army fire engine), crewed by army troops, were sent to deal with a blaze while firefighters were still on strike. Since the firefighters' strike began, 119 people had died as a result. The year ended with the release of *Star Wars*, a film that had been a massive hit in the United States. It was screened in British cinemas for the first time over the Christmas period. On Christmas Day, the UK public settled down to watch traditional comedy duo Morecambe and Wise present their Christmas show to an audience of more than twenty-eight million viewers.

In September, *Voyager 1* was launched into space by the United States, and a nuclear non-proliferation pact was signed by fifteen countries, including the Soviet Union and the United States. Pelé played his final professional football (soccer) game in October. Irish American gangster Danny Greene was murdered by a car bomb during a gangland killing in Ohio. Four gay rights activists threw pies at antigay campaigner Anita Bryant during a press conference in Iowa, which resulted in her abandoning her antigay stance. Three members of the Southern rock band Lynyrd Skynyrd died in a plane crash in Mississippi, just three days after the release of their fifth album, *Street Survivors*. Meat Loaf released his massively successful album *Bat Out of Hell*. In November, the people of San Francisco elected Harvey Milk as city supervisor. He was the first openly gay elected official in any US city. In December, the charter plane carrying the University of Evansville basketball team crashed in dense fog, killing twenty-nine people. Also in December, a massive dust storm hit Southern California, killing three people and causing $40 million in damages.

OTHER PISTOLS HAPPENINGS

Malcolm McLaren was working on the Sex Pistols movie, which was to be titled *Who Killed Bambi*. The film was to star 1960s pop star and girlfriend of Mick Jagger, Marianne Faithful, and was to have a budget of £750,000. However, one of the financial backers of the film pulled out in November 1977, leaving the future of the movie in question (Wood 1988). The Sex Pistols began a tour of radio stations to promote their new album, and they also made a series of personal appearances at Virgin Record stores, including shops in Nottingham, Sheffield, Liverpool, and Glasgow. Plans were being put in place for a major UK tour in March 1978.

In December, the *Sun* newspaper ran a front-page story titled "Sex Pistol and Girl in Drugs Probe" discussing how Sid Vicious and his girlfriend, Nancy Spungen, were arrested. In the end, no charges were made (Wood 1988). The band, particularly Johnny Rotten, were increasingly worried about Sid's relationship with Nancy. Nancy and Sid were becoming inseparable, and she was influencing Sid, particularly in terms of his drug use.

The Sex Pistols embarked on a short tour of Holland, including shows in Rotterdam, Maastricht, Tilburg, Arnhem, Eindhoven, Groningen, Maasbree, and Wimschoten.

CONCLUSION

The impact of *Never Mind the Bollocks, Here's the Sex Pistols* is undeniable. The rock music climate had become safe, boring, bland, complacent, dull, and pathetic (Poulsen 2005). Popular music was crying out for the danger, passion, and shock that, in one slab of pure rock 'n' roll, the Pistols' album provided. Johnny Rotten and the band came crashing through a year of musical stagnation and economic and social decline, talking directly to youth that were ready for a new voice. In many ways, punk placed Britain firmly back on the musical map, and London was seen as the place to be. Several US bands, including Johnny Thunders and the Heartbreakers, Cherry Vanilla, and Wayne County, had already relocated to London. The Pistols' album solidified UK punk as the new musical phenomenon.

8

CHRISTMAS WITH THE PISTOLS

December 1977

The winter of 1977/78 was cold and bleak. Union action continued because of the imposition of a 5 percent maximum pay increase for public service workers at a time when inflation was running at 15 percent. The thirty-thousand-strong firefighters' union lodged a 30 percent pay demand, ordering their workers out on strike, and the army was called in to provide emergency cover. In the private sector, the UK's auto industry was experiencing a disastrous year, with foreign cars outselling British-built ones for the first time. The UK comedy trio The Goodies captured the mood of the time perfectly in their Christmas TV show "Earthanasia," or "The End of the World Show." Set in a single room, The Goodies watched as the world was ending from pollution, inflation, overpopulation, and racism and planned how best to spend their last minutes of life. The following year, 1978, was not to be any better, culminating in a "Winter of Discontent," with widespread strikes, a vote of no confidence in the Labour government, and ultimately a general election won by the Conservative Party.

The Pistols remained hungry to perform, particularly as new recruit Sid was now starting to play bass much better, and embarked on another short "Never Mind the Bans" series of "guerrilla gigs" across the United Kingdom in December 1977. At short notice just as the tour started, a full-page advertisement appeared in the *New Musical Express*. It showed crosses on a map but no locations or dates. This was to be the Sex Pistols' final tour of the United Kingdom, playing their last gig in their home country at Ivanhoe's nightclub in Huddersfield on Christmas Day 1977. They played two shows that day, an afternoon show for kids of striking firefighters and an evening show for the general public. The concerts were filmed "on a big old crappy U-matic low-band camera" by Julien Temple that was featured in a video titled *Never Mind the Baubles*. The film shows Johnny Rotten playing Santa and handing out badges, posters, and Christmas goodie bags. The band had great fun playing for the firefighters' kids, in what must have been an almost surreal event, complete with party cake fights and funny party hats. Four days before the Christmas concert, four children died in a house fire, as poorly prepared troops attempted to deal with a blaze while the firefighters were on strike.

This chapter tracks the final UK tour, discussing its political and social importance and how the Christmas Day concerts show another side of the punk band. It will unpick the relationship between the punk message, the political climate, and the firefighters' strike, set against the backdrop of a severe winter of fuel shortages, blizzards, and industrial unrest.

THE FIREFIGHTERS' STRIKE

During the winter of 1977, England was gripped in a national emergency caused by a firefighters' strike. The strike began on November 14 and lasted for nine weeks, until January 1978. The firefighters were demanding a 30 percent pay raise, which had been turned down by the government. At the time, firefighters were paid an average of £71 per week, while the national average earnings were £79. This strike joined a number of other organizations that were also striking, such as print workers, journalists, and network engineers. These strikes caused national newspapers such as the *Daily Mirror* and *The Sun* and television channels including the BBC, to be out of operation.

In order to deal with this national emergency, the government ordered ten thousand personnel from the army, air force, and navy to provide emergency cover. The firefighters locked the stations, so army personnel had to resort to using outdated "Green Goddess" engines. Green Goddess engines were held by the armed forces in reserve for national emergencies. They were very old-fashioned, many dating back to the early 1950s—hardly state-of-the-art technology.

The strike started to take hold in November 1977 and people were keeping buckets of sand and water in their homes in case of a fire. The London Fire Brigade developed a safety guide that was issued nationally and advised people to check for smouldering cigarettes and unplug electrical appliances when not in use. It wasn't long before the strike had a real impact and led to tragedies. On November 21, 1977, two children died in a house fire in London. Andrew Stephen, reporting for the *Sunday Telegraph*, spent the day with the army crew working on a Green Goddess and said: "Everyone realises only too well that with their primitive equipment the soldiers will be hopelessly ill-equipped to deal with a big fire."

It took until January 1978 before a settlement was reached. The firefighters finally agreed to a 10 percent pay rise with guarantees of future increases. They went back to work on January 16, 1978. The dispute had been a costly one in many ways; bad feelings remained, and lives had been lost. Fire damage cost £117 million compared to £52 million in the same three months of the previous year.

A TOUR OF HOLLAND

The ongoing relationship between Sid Vicious and Nancy Spungen continued to concern Malcolm McLaren and the band. On December 1, *The Sun* ran a front-page story titled "Sex Pistol and Girl in Drugs Probe" that described how Sid and Nancy had been arrested on suspicion of possession of drugs. In the end, no charges were filed; however, the event raised further concerns with the band and management. There was a foiled attempt by the Pistols' management to kidnap Nancy and send her back to New York. The attempt was semi-serious, but failed.

Also at the beginning of December, the Sex Pistols embarked on a short tour of Holland, opening at the Eksit Club in Rotterdam. It consisted of nine dates with the band returning to Rotterdam for the final show. They opened with "God Save the Queen" and played almost everything that they had ever recorded, along with the new song "Belsen Was a Gas" and the old song "Flowers of Romance." Sid declares that it was the "best gig the Sex Pistols have ever played" (Wood 1988). The band was pleased to be playing again; unfortunately, a tour of Finland that was planned for early 1978 had to be canceled because the Pistols were denied work permits.

NEVER MIND THE BANS TOUR

The Sex Pistols were keen to get out and play in their home country again and a short tour of clubs in the United Kingdom was set up. A full-page ad ran in the music papers with the headline "Never Mind the Bans," showing a series of newspaper clippings about previous concerts that had been canceled due to bans. At the bottom of the page was a promise: "Sex Pistols Will Play December Tour 77." No dates were listed as a precaution in case shows were canceled.

The tour would eventually consist of ten dates, including two on Christmas Day in Ivanhoe's in Huddersfield. The tour opened with a concert at Brunel University, Uxbridge, London, on December 16 followed by a gig at Mr Georges in Coventry the following evening. The Pistols were then off to Wolverhampton to play a gig at Lafayettes on December 18 and then the following day to play at the Nikkers Club in Keighley.

I was keen to see the Sex Pistols live in concert again and telephoned several of the likely venues to ask if the band was playing there. I managed to find out most of the dates and realized that the closest was the Keighley gig. I telephoned Nikkers and asked if I could buy tickets for the concert and was told by the receptionist that "the Sex Pistols are playing here for the people of Keighley. If you want tickets you will have to come to the club and buy them. Oh, and by the way we only have a few tickets left." I asked her to hold two tickets for me as I had a one-hundred-mile drive to the club. However, she refused to do so. In the end, I decided to give the gig a miss, a decision I regret to this day, given this was to be my last chance to see the Sex Pistols.

The remaining dates of the tour were December 20 at the Hamilton Club in Birkenhead, December 22 at Champness Hall in Rochdale, December 23 at Newport Village, December 24 at Links Pavilion in Cromer, and on Christmas Day two concerts at Ivanhoe's in Huddersfield. This was to be the last tour of the United Kingdom by the Sex Pistols until reunion shows that would take place many years later.

CLUB LAFAYETTE, WOLVERHAMPTON

Peter Don't Care (1977) was lucky enough to attend the gig in Wolverhampton. He has kindly allowed me to reproduce his review of the gig below. His vivid account conveys the excitement of seeing the Sex Pistols in 1977.

> The club was still filling when Satan's Rats the support group hit the stage. They were a mixture of high energy pop and new wave, very energetic and a good warm up for the audience. As Satan's Rats left the stage, the club atmosphere grew increasingly intense as the time wore on and everybody anticipated what was about to follow. You have to remember the Pistols at this stage in their career were the number one band [and banned] in the land. They were headline news everywhere. Only a few days previous Johnny Rotten was on the front page of the *Daily Mirror* cos he pulled out the earlier date booked for tonight's performance cos he had a cold!!! If Johnny had gone to the dentist he would've made the papers!!! It was now getting uncomfortably packed. There were even queues for the toilets of this small club, what held about 400–500 tops. And it was ten deep at both upstairs and downstairs bars. Everyone seemed to have had the same idea, stock up now while you can before "they" come on. Cos no-one wanted to miss the notorious freak show when it hits town! There were all walks of life in here tonight . . . the fans, the curious and the twisted all wanting a glimpse of something extraordinary. The DJ kept on saying "after this next record the Sex Pistols will appear live on stage." This went on for at least 3 spins of the Stranglers, the Clash and Eddie And the Hot Rods or some other band. While all this was going on people were crowding around the stage area vying for position. The stage door kept on swinging open and shut as roadies made final adjustments to the gear and every time it opened for a brief second you could see Johnny Rotten drinking from a can laughing. I asked the DJ one more time when they were really coming on and he said, "'he didn't know what the hold-up was!"

Then smack on the stroke of midnight the white stage lights went up and they just walked on unannounced. The crowd went wild as Johnny sneered "Hello Wolverhampton" as they careered straight into "God Save The Queen." What other song could they start with? There was pandemonium everywhere rebounding all around the club and the seething masses were swaying like a football crowd. . . . You could see the glassiness in Johnny's laser beam eye and seeing the Pistols in the flesh lived up to the what I had expected and more. . . . Johnny Rotten an arm's length away scrutinises the crowd with a demented stare as he informs us there is "no future, no future for you!" He is decked out with a smattering of talcum powder rubbed into his dirty yellow spiky barnet and covering the shoulders of his black suit jacket. . . . His baggy blue tartan bondage strides were rounded off with a pair of the brightest red brothel creepers you've ever seen. It took a few seconds before the shellshock opening had sunk in. You've got to remember this was the real thing! The band we had read about, heard about this was the Pistols!!! The group were sipping lager from packs of cans littering the amps and floor of the stage. And with no time to hang around it signalled the next number "I Wanna Be Me" which got Sid pogoing with his bass going all over the shop. Yeah . . . before he then decided on having a gobbing match with one of the punters. Sid dressed in his black leather and Levi's was leering over at the crowd not concentrating quite so much on his beloved bass playing as he should've but it was all done in a joking banter. And Sid was first to remonstrate with the bouncers as they moved in, causing a slight scuffle and ejected his unfortunate sparring partner from the club. Not the first and by no means the last to see the street lights prematurely tonight. Whilst all this was going on I noticed Sid's bird the "Nauseating Nancy" was standing at the back of the stage leaning against the back wall next to the little door that leads to the tiny dressing room. She was drinking, smoking and chewing gum, watching Sid all the time with her arms folded.

Halfway through "Seventeen" and Johnny's mic-stand topples over amid the confusion of mic-lead and Johnny's energy. It falls straight into the no-man's land of scaffold bars and debris between the baying crowd and the public enemy number one. John resumes singing with no stand to throw around while Rodent scurries over from stage left behind Sid's amp and recovers it. He crouches down in front of John trying not to get soaked by the various beer and gob ridden missiles hitting the stage at regular intervals. John laughs!

And declares "This ain't the Wolverhampton I used to know!" "New York" is up next and there certainly ain't no imitations on stage tonight! This is the real thing! To see them perform no more than 3ft away (which is still something I will never get over) is something else, larger than life. Whatever you read about 'em in the papers they were so much better and probably worse! "EMI" blasts out at us with Steve Jones shouting the chorus in his wideboy cockney accent, as he rips out those power chords on his infamous white Gibson. He seems to love every minute of this performance as he lurches around in his leather and tatty black creepers but does he care? does he f°°k! As the set progresses in what seems like the blink of an eye the grinding chords of "Submission" welcomes in a barrage of objects from all corners of the audience. Anything from jumpers, scarves, shirts, hats and bits of rubbish with quickly scrawled messages on like "F°°K OFF!" and other friendly gestures hit the expanse of the 18-ft. stage. "Bodies" steams in next and really gets an over active response from the crowd. At the climax Johnny gathers up a lot of this new stage wear he's acquired into a pile in his arms and cradles 'em in his jacket like you would a baby laughing with glee as he yelps "mommm-meeeeeeah!" There is a minute or so pause as the stage is now inundated with jumble sale attire. Johnny starts trying on various items as Paul Cook starts pounding the intro to "Holidays in The Sun." You can hardly see Paul behind his black drum kit but you can certainly hear him. He only stops to have a drink or two or to wipe the perspiration from his face. Good old Cooky (ha ha ha). All through "Holidays . . ." Johnny Rotten is trying on his new gear and throwing it off for more obnoxious stuff. In the end, he sticks with what he's got on, wise move! He kicks a few of the cast-off jumpers into the bass drum and mutters "them'll do for after." He then announces, "this next un's gonna be our new single" just as Steve Jones rings out the sinister chords to "Belsen Was a Gas." Me or anyone else could barely make this new song out as John was prancing from one side of the stage to the other "ha ha-ing" as he went. He seemed to get off on this one nearly as much as "God Save The Queen". But just before "No Feelings" gets despatched, a pint glass was thrown from the audience, it just missed Paul Cook's drum kit by inches and shattered on impact against the wall at the back of the stage. John sarcastically threw a gauntlet down by announcing "Whoever threw that, would they like to make their presence felt up here now!" The crowd cheered! Paul Cook didn't seem disturbed, he was probably used to such happenings with this band. And he knew it wasn't really meant for him anyway! The Pistols trod a very dangerous path looking back on it now. They caused some wild reactions everywhere they went good and bad! Wolverhampton at this time was full of nutters and a nasty place to be.

But it was soon back to the business of the night with a more inflamed "No Feelings." As Mr. Rotten gave us a dose of stage theatrics by pretending to hang himself from the lighting rig above his head (by wrapping the mic lead around his neck!) A few of us stuck our hands out, mine included, and we got the shake the hand of the geezer who was supposedly the devil incarnate. This might sound stupid now but at the time was something f°°king out of this world!!! I was proud to be here at this particular moment in time and shake hands with the Anti-Christ! One kid dropped his cigarettes after offering John a fag and he couldn't reach them. Johnny bent down and handed the packet back to the kid! Was this the Johnny Rotten portrayed in the papers!? On the side of the stage there were a few snaps of cameras going off. I noticed one Japanese photographer getting some great shots. I always wondered where they ended up? What I'd give to see them now!!! Back to the gig. Sid had draped his leather over the amps by now revealing four or five nasty cuts to his chest, self-inflicted of course! The familiar chords of "Pretty Vacant" ring out the PA system. This is played brilliantly by Jonesey who had dispelled all the myths about not playing well. Cos, they played brilliantly on every number tonight!! And whipped the crowd up into a frenzy. As a hoarse Johnny Rotten screamed down the mic "and we don't carreee!!!" There was no way I was vacating my position now stuck behind this big fat punkette who kept elbowing me in the stomach all night! She was soon just a mild irritation as the power chords of everyone's favourite "Anarchy" erupted out the PA system. We'd been waiting all night for this one and it came blaring into our eardrums "Right nowwwww!!!" In the mass of sweat and body heat the club erupts for what seemed like the biggest earthquake of the night. I take a glance around the club amid the furore and everyone and I mean everyone upstairs and downstairs, bar staff, security you name it, the whole f°°king club is transfixed to the stage! Long haired students, yobs, punks, straights you name it they all know this one. And it's being sung from everyone's lips. I dunno where he gets it from but Johnny is moving around like a madman, jerking and falling over. Then before I can take it all in the lights go out!!! And the last I see is Paul Cook's back disappearing through the small blue dressing room door. They were gone and there was no encore!!!! As I slowly stagger out the club in the p°°°ing rain I didn't care. I was already soaked with sweat and adrenaline and my ears are still ringing! I knew I'd just been present at something special. Little did I know at the time I had just witnessed a musical phenomenon and had encountered the best sixty minutes I will probably ever have in my entire life!! It's one of those sights and experiences that remains with ya for the rest of your natural! SEX PISTOLS WON'T PLAY! THEY SURE F°°KING DID TONIGHT! Peter Don't Care.

BELSEN WAS A GAS

The controversial song "Belsen Was a Gas" was becoming a regular feature of the Sex Pistols' live set. The song was designed to offend, particularly the older generation who had grown up during World War II and for whom the Holocaust was still a terrible memory. Belsen was a concentration camp where particularly terrible atrocities took place and the very mention of it was upsetting to those who had lived through the war. The song was credited to the whole band, but it had been written by Sid Vicious a couple of years before when he was in his early band, the Flowers of Romance. It was originally intended to be a joke, the title being a pun on the gas that was used to kill Jews in the Nazi concentration camps. Sid often used Nazi symbolism for its shock value, often wearing a swastika armband. John Lydon later admitted that the song was in bad taste in an interview for *Q* magazine (in 1996) he said: "['Belsen Was a Gas'] was a very nasty, silly little thing. . . . That should've ended up on the cutting room floor."

   The song did not appear on the Sex Pistols' debut album; however, it did appear on the soundtrack album for the movie *The Great Rock 'n' Roll Swindle* and was performed by Public Image Limited (John Lydon's post-Pistols band) and the Sex Pistols themselves at some of their later reunion shows. The song even became "Baghdad Was a Blast" after the start of the Iraq War, during a reunion tour of the United States in 2003.

CHRISTMAS DAY 1977

But the Sex Pistols had something special planned for Christmas. On Christmas Day, the tour reached the Yorkshire town of Huddersfield in the North of England. Rather than their normal club gig, the Pistols planned two shows at Ivanhoe's: an afternoon show for the children of striking firefighters, and an evening show for the firefighters themselves and older punters. In a somewhat surreal event, the most hated and feared punk band in the country played a matinee concert to young children with cakes, food, and Christmas presents from the band. With little or no money coming into the firefighters' homes, and food on ration, this was a welcome addition to their meager Christmas celebrations.

These Christmas benefit gigs were organized quietly and secretly between the Sex Pistols and the Fire Brigade Union. Secrecy was of the utmost importance because if the local council discovered that the Sex Pistols were due to play at Ivanhoe's, the concerts would undoubtedly have been canceled. Johnny Rotten recalls: "Huddersfield I remember very fondly. Two concerts, a matinee with children throwing pies at me, and later that night, striking union members. It was heaven. There was a lot of love in the house. It was great that day, everything about it. Just wonderful." Drummer Paul Cook recalls: "It was like our Christmas party really. We remember everyone being really relaxed that day, everyone was getting on really well, everyone was in such a great mood because it was a benefit for the kids of firemen who were on strike at that time, who had been on strike for a long time" (Gallagher 2013).

Jez Scott, who attended the matinee as a young boy, wrote about the gig in *The Guardian*:

> Johnny Rotten came out in a straw hat and they had a cake with Sex Pistols written on it, the size of a car bonnet. He started cutting it up but it soon degenerated into a food fight. He was covered head to foot. It was fantastic. I took a photo of Steve Jones, who did a rock'n'roll-type pose. I took one of Sid and he asked, "Do you want to Put Nancy [Spungen] in as well?"
>
> Eventually, the Pistols came onstage. I think they only played about six songs. I remember they did "Bodies," but omitted the swear words because of the children. Steve Jones's guitar sounded very raw and exciting. During "Holidays in the Sun," Rotten held out

the mic and people were shouting out their names, but because I was probably the only punk there I tried to shout the lyrics: "Cheap dialogue/Cheap essential scenery."

The gig itself was great. Sid had his leather jacket open and was hammering the bass. They were really on form and I was a bit overcome, really. I'd taken my album along but I was so excited talking to the Pistols, I forgot to get it signed. Sid was the easiest to talk to because he was like one of us, like a kid. I asked him what he was doing next and he said they were going to America. I'd like to think I said, "Don't go, it'll all go pear-shaped," but I didn't. Within a few weeks the band had split, Sid had been remanded for murdering Nancy and then he died. I wore a black tie with a Sex Pistols badge on it for a year in mourning.

The two Huddersfield concerts were captured on film by Julien Temple and eventually surfaced in the BBC documentary "Never Mind the Baubles," which was screened on UK television in 2013. The documentary shows the Pistols at their best. Sadly, this was to be their last UK concert. The band would travel to the United States in early 1978 and implode. The documentary "Never Mind the Baubles" was reviewed in *TimeOut*:

> Apparently Julien Temple has had footage of the final pair of British Sex Pistols gigs—performed on Christmas Day 1977 to the children of striking Huddersfield firefighters and then in the evening, to their parents—knocking around for ages. We're glad he's finally decided to share it with the world, because it's a thrilling and surprisingly touching treat. Essentially, at Huddersfield's Ivanhoe's club, the mask slipped and the then-bogeymen of British music allowed themselves to be seen for what they really were: a combative, disorderly but essentially good-hearted bunch of lads. Furthermore, seeing the Pistols performing to kids comes close to actually unearthing some fresh insight into the band; as the experience seems to have done for John Lydon himself. Basically, the youngsters get it, instinctively understanding the purity, sincerity, and under-appreciated comedy of the band. And, mainly at the instigation of Lydon himself, they respond by throwing a lot of cake. It's a beautiful story in the most traditional festive sense imaginable; two groups of righteous outcasts finding unlikely solace in each other on Christmas day. "It deeply affected me," says Lydon. And the look on his face suggests he means every word. (Harrison 2013)

MEANWHILE ... OUT IN THE PROVINCES

The year 1977 was when punk rock started to grow all around the United Kingdom with local bands and local venues establishing themselves. In my area, the North East of England, several new punk bands were gigging, notably Penetration and the Angelic Upstarts. The major venue for punk rock was Middlesbrough Rock Garden. In the following sections, I recount some gigs I attended in 1977 and how these bands illustrate the growth and importance of punk rock within the North East of England and how they were influenced directly by the major punk bands including the Sex Pistols and The Clash.

Penetration was the most well established, and in my view, the best 1970s North East punk band. They were big fans of, and directly influenced by, the Sex Pistols. I attended lots of their gigs from early 1977 onward. They all blur into one now, but what I do remember clearly are some great songs, and Pauline Murray's performance, which was always stunning. I recall listening to an early track, "Duty Free Technology," on the radio for the first time and thinking how great it was that local guys had made it. I got to know all the early tracks well before any were released on vinyl. Pauline and the rest of the original band (Gary Chaplin, Rob Blamire, and Gary Smallman) frequented punk gigs in Newcastle and the Rock Garden. The way in which they caught early Pistols gigs and how that influenced them to form the band is well-documented (Robb 2006). Penetration was, in turn, a big influence on the North East music scene. They built up a solid following locally and gigged all over the country, becoming quite a "name" band.

The Bedrock Festival took place the first weekend of July 1977. It was part of the broader Newcastle Festival activities: a weekend devoted to local rock talent. The venue was the University Theatre, which is a small hall next to Newcastle University. The Friday lunchtime gig was devoted to punk and moved at the last minute to the dining hall of Newcastle Polytechnic because the University Theatre made a policy decision to pull out of any punk rock gigs; such was the paranoia of the time. The venue wasn't full; a small grouping of punks, rock fans, and students gathered to enjoy the music of a couple of local bands. Harry Hack and the Big G were first, followed by Penetration, who were starting to build up their own following. Both bands put on a good show, but my memories are of Penetration, who had assembled a set of strong, self-penned songs, which became the tracks on their first album, *Moving Targets*, released the following year. My early favorites were "Silent Community," "Firing Squad" (later a single), and Pauline's great treatment of Patti Smith's "Free Money."

Alex Baxter recalls Penetration playing an early Middlesbrough Rock Garden gig: "an agile, powerful band who had the then-unusual distinction of being female-fronted. The night I saw them, lead singer Pauline dedicated a song to a lad who had decked his arm with safety pins through the flesh, their war-cry: "Don't Dictate," and I think the irony may have been lost on him" (Delplanque 2010).

The importance of local bands, including Penetration, Harry Hack and the Big G, Blitzkrieg Bob, and the Angelic Upstarts, in the development of punk culture in the North East cannot be overstated. Gigs by these bands formed rallying points for punks across the region to come together and celebrate their new identity and enjoy new music. They were also often the scene of violent clashes between punks, skinheads, and rock fans, and between fans and security staff. Phil Sutcliffe (1979) reported a "fracas" at a Penetration gig at Newcastle City Hall in which "over-aggressive bouncers drove a section of the crowd on to the stage" causing an otherwise peaceful and highly enjoyable concert to "close amid some chaos" with seats smashed and at Penetration being banned from the City Hall.

Peter Howard of Harry Hack and the Big G states, "Punk was a bit of a shock to a lot of people in the North. At the . . . pub . . . we were all banned for life because one of us was wearing a skeleton earring . . . . another gig . . . after the first song, the manager marched up and pulled the plug . . . students who'd been watching invited us to finish the gig . . . at the [students'] union" (Butcher 2012). In the same article, Howard also raises the DIY nature of North East punk: "We couldn't afford Vivienne Westwood up here and the whole punk thing was far more of a home-made affair than the London scene."

Middlesbrough is a large town situated on the south bank of the River Tees. The local economy is dominated by the nearby chemical industry. The Rock Garden in Newport Road, Middlesbrough, was *the* venue for punk rock in the North East. Everyone (the Sex Pistols, The Clash, The Damned, Adam and the Ants, 999) played there. It was an old bier keller, which is basically a room with a stage, a bar, a few tables and benches, and a small kitchen. They served the best burgers I have ever tasted. As the years went on, the gigs started to attract more and more local punks and skins and were often marred by violence. Alex Baxter recalls (Delplanque 2010): "In my teenage years, I was a regular at the Rock Garden, a small, rather dingy venue on Newport Road which catered for the rock music crowd, and was next door to the more sophisticated Marimba, a club aimed at the 'supper set' with its light, easy listening style entertainment. There was nothing 'easy' about the listening at the Rock Garden, however." It was actually a very dangerous place to visit. Every time I went, I felt in fear of violence, and there were fights at almost every gig I attended.

The Rock Garden continued to host gigs into the early 1980s. However, "major fashion chains were stocking skinny jeans, zip and safety pin encrusted t-shirts and more 'straight' people were adopting the spiky hairstyles once unique to punk" and Alex Baxter, like many others (including myself) decided that "it was time to check out" (Delplanque 2010). The venue was very much of its time, but was an important and vital part of the North East punk scene.

The Angelic Upstarts hailed from South Shields. The original lineup was Mensi (vocals), Mond (guitar), Steve Forsten (bass), and Decca Wade (drums). Mensi worked as a miner; punk was his escape route from the pits. In an interview for *Redstar73* fanzine (2006), he explains how "his childhood had been a totally working-class type background; being brought up on Labour politics, considering the Tories as an enemy." Mond worked in the shipyard as an electrician. The band had been influenced by seeing The Clash at Newcastle University: "It was after the White Riot tour. We were basically all from the same council estate and basically it was me going around, knocking on the doors asking if anybody could play an instrument. They were the first ones I found who could play something, actually strum a note. I couldn't play f**k all, so I said, 'Right, I'm the f**king singer, then'" (PunkyGibbon 2017).

Their concerts were legendary, partly because of the hardcore troublemakers who came along, and their controversial stage act. An Upstarts gig had an atmosphere of its own. The audience would be strongly committed fans, mostly skinheads and punks (more skinheads as time went on) who bought into the Upstarts socialist and anti-establishment philosophy. Their manager, cum bouncer and miner, was local hard man and ex-boxing champ Keith Bell, better known as "The Sheriff." He could be found in front of the stage at their gigs, always ready to jump into the crowd and sort out any fights. Bell went to prison in 1980 for arson (Fitzsimons 2013).

There were often fights at Upstarts gigs. I always lurked around the back of the hall, feeling quite exposed as one of the few people in the audience with long hair. Their set at the time consisted of "Student Power" ("What a Shower" according to the lyrics; "F**king Shower" live), "Small Town Small Mind," "Police Oppression," and the song that was always a highlight and became their anthem, "The Murder of Liddle Towers." Liddle Towers was a local amateur boxer who died following a spell while in police custody in 1976. An inquest into his death returned a verdict of justifiable homicide. The Upstarts song told the story: "Who killed Liddle? The police killed Liddle." The track is a great slab of raw punk; amazingly powerful live. At early gigs, Mensi would introduce the song by bringing on stage a whole pig's head, which he had purchased at the butchers that day. The pig's head would have a policeman's hat perched on top of it and Mensi would hold it aloft to great cheers from the crowd. The song would start and he would throw the head into the mosh pit. The audience would kick the head around the floor, throw it about the place, and generally go crazy. I have an enduring memory of a skinhead biting the ears of the pig's head. While this was going on, Mensi was screaming and growling the lyrics, wearing the policeman's hat.

Phil Sutcliffe (1978) reviewed an Angelic Upstarts gig in *Sounds* and wrote of "young music screaming for change with no chance of reaching a mass audience except by leasing itself to multinational capital" and declared the band "dangerous" and their performance "barbaric instinctive theatre teetering on the edge of chaos." He goes on to discuss how the North was in some ways "getting there a year too late." The Upstarts drew from their own local politics, writing and singing about "living local issues," which meant so much to them particularly as they "haven't seen much yet outside a ten-mile radius from the council estate they grew up on" (Sutcliffe 1978).

The Sex Pistols played relatively few concerts in the North East. However, the importance of those few gigs cannot be underestimated. Early Pistols gigs in the region were life changing for a small number of people (including myself), shocking and annoying to some, yet insignificant to most. Later gigs reaffirmed the Pistols position as the premier punk band and were amazing experiences that will be remembered forever.

MOVING INTO 1978

The Sex Pistols ended 1977 on a high. The Never Mind the Bans tour was a big success, providing unforgettable experiences for the small number of lucky fans who witnessed the band at their best. The Pistols were soon to embark on a tour of the United States, which sadly was to be their last. The events of the US tour are discussed in the next, and final, chapter of the Sex Pistols' story.

9

EVER GET THE FEELING YOU'VE BEEN CHEATED?

January 1978

It was 1978 in the United Kingdom, a new year, but not much had changed. It was still a country locked in an atmosphere of discontent. On the positive side, on January 16, the firefighters' strike ended with their acceptance of a 10 percent pay raise and reduced working hours. On January 18, the European Court of Human Rights found the British government guilty of the mistreatment of prisoners in Northern Ireland, and at the end of the month, Margaret Thatcher, the leader of the Conservative Party (who was in opposition to the Labor government) said that many British people fear being "swamped by people with a different culture." At the end of the month, eighteen-year-old prostitute Helen Rytka was murdered in the northern Yorkshire town of Huddersfield, making her the eighth victim of the notorious Yorkshire Ripper.

In the United States, the "Great Blizzard of 1978" hit the Ohio Valley and the Great Lakes, killing more than fifty people. The blizzard also struck New England and New York, where it killed approximately one hundred people and caused more than $520 million in damage. On January 28, Richard Chase, the famous "Vampire of Sacramento," was arrested. Chase killed six people and infamously drank their blood and cannibalized their remains. Hollywood film director Roman Polanski

fled to France to avoid being sentenced after pleading guilty to unlaw-
ful sex with a minor.

In the world of the Sex Pistols, much was about to change. Malcolm
McLaren had been planning for some time for the band to tour the
United States. The planning of the tour was surreal from the outset.
Rather than book concerts in major "rock" cities like New York and Los
Angeles, McLaren decided to target the Deep South. He booked the
Sex Pistols to play shows in Atlanta, Memphis, San Antonio, Baton
Rouge, Dallas, and Tulsa. The tour was to end in San Francisco, which
was the only major city where the audience was likely to welcome the
British punk band. The dates were set up from the start to ensure
maximum culture clash, confrontation, and media interest.

The tour was originally scheduled to start shortly before New Year's;
however, it was delayed because US authorities did not wish to issue
visas to some of the band members because they had criminal records.
This resulted in the first few dates of the tour being canceled. The tour
dates were:

- January 5, 1978, Great Southeast Music Hall, Atlanta, Georgia
- January 6, 1978, Taliesyn Ballroom, Memphis, Tennessee
- January 8, 1978, Randy's Rodeo, San Antonio, Texas
- January 9,1978, Kingfish Club, Baton Rouge, Louisiana
- January 10, 1978, Longhorn Ballroom, Dallas, Texas
- January 12, 1978, Cain's Ballroom, Tulsa, Oklahoma
- January 14, 1978, Winterland Ballroom, San Francisco, California

There was much media interest about the tour, and punk and new wave
fans in the United States were hungry to see the legendary UK leaders
of punk rock. However, the venues, which were largely redneck bars,
were bound to create and provoke hostile reactions to the Sex Pistols.
Malcolm McLaren later went on to admit that he had purposely booked
the band into these odd venues to create maximum trouble, violence,
and impact (Crabtree 2004).

The tour did not get off to a good start. Sid Vicious was heavily
addicted to heroin and beginning to believe, and live up to, his own
caricature image as the ultimate punk rock star. John Lydon later con-
fessed that Sid "finally had an audience of people who would be here
with shock and horror. . . . Sid was easily led by the nose" (Lydon and

Zimmerman 1995). John tried to stay close to Sid throughout the tour as an attempt to keep him away from drugs. However, as soon as they hit a major city, Sid would disappear and score. For example, this happened early in the tour when Sid disappeared from the Holiday Inn in Memphis, Tennessee, where the band was staying, searching for drugs. He was later found in the local hospital with the words "Gimme a fix" written across his chest in black magic marker.

THE OPENING SHOW

The tour began on January 5, 1978, at the Great Southeast Music Hall in Atlanta, Georgia. They exploded onto the stage and opened with "God Save the Queen," followed by "I Wanna Be Me," "17," and "New York." The short set continued with "Bodies," "Submission," "Holidays in the Sun," "EMI," "No Feelings," "Problems," and "Pretty Vacant." The final song was an explosive "Anarchy in the UK."

Atlanta was a well-established center of country music, beginning as early as the 1920s, and by the 1970s it was also the center for Southern rock with bands such as the Allman Brothers and Lynyrd Skynyrd. However, there was also a growing punk rock scene by the time the Sex Pistols played there. Having said that, country music and Southern rock were still the mainstay of the music scene in Atlanta. As a result, the audience consisted of people who were there out of curiosity, and many that attended purely to cause trouble. Members of the band were not getting along that well, and as a result, the tour was plagued by infighting and very hostile audience reactions.

According to Henry (2008), the Sex Pistols' visit to Atlanta provided a catalyst for the punk rock scene in the city. Prior to the Pistols playing Atlanta, people were listening to punk, and some new bands had started up, but there was no real punk scene (Henry 2008). The Sex Pistols' concert was unlike anything the city had seen before. Sid Vicious appeared without a shirt and wearing tight black jeans, while Johnny Rotten looked disheveled, wearing an open vest covered with buttons and a loosely knotted tie (Henry 2008). "The Sex Pistols brought a distilled version of punk to Atlanta," according to Danny Beard. "After that show, you saw people wearing leather and dressing differently." Jill Griffin agreed: "From that point on, everybody wanted to be punk.

They cut their hair and got skinny ties and stopped wearing bell bottoms" (Henry 2008).

The reality was that very few people actually attended the show; only about five hundred people packed into the small venue, and many of them were journalists who came from all over the United States to see the punk sensation. The atmosphere in the hall was strange. Rather than the traditional pogoing and spitting, the band was showered with a strange collection of items, including pig's trotters (i.e., feet) (Monk and Gutterman 1990). According to Henry (2008), local groupie Griffin and a friend took Sid Vicious home after the show where he "spent the night ransacking a medicine cabinet and trying to cut his wrist with a letter opener." Meanwhile, Malcolm McLaren went searching for Sid. When he found the bassist, he took him to the local hospital where his arm was bandaged. He was now ready for the next gig.

Ken Hutson (2014) commented, "I went to this show mostly out of curiosity. I was by myself because most of friends didn't think much of the punk scene. I was more intrigued than interested. I stood at the back of the hall. It was a very intense hour. There were some moments when you thought the whole place would erupt in well, anarchy. So as a singer with friends in music this became the jumping off point for our future with punk/new wave and we migrated from late '70s arena rock to Club 688 in downtown Atlanta."

The following excerpt, "When the Sex Pistols Came to Memphis," is taken from Graves (2015). The excerpt also appears on the www.guerrillamonsterfilms.com site of Mike McCarthy. Many thanks indeed to Tom Graves for letting me reprint this chapter.

When the Sex Pistols Came to Memphis

When the Sex Pistols blitzed into Memphis on a very cold Friday night in January (the 6th) 1978 probably not one in ten people in the audience had ever heard one note of their music. Only days before the concert Warner Brothers Records released their atom bomb of a record, *Never Mind the Bollocks, Here's the Sex Pistols*, stateside in a hot pink cover with the iconic torn graphics that came to symbolize everything about the British punk movement. Prior to that the Sex Pistols had received no airplay in Memphis and an import version of their LP, which had a Dayglo yellow cover instead of hot pink, was available at none of the Memphis-area record shops.

A tiny section in the back of Peaches Records on Park Avenue had some imported singles and it was there that I found "Pretty Vacant," as far as I know the only Sex Pistols anything that was available prior to the news that the most controversial band in history—way more reviled than Elvis, the Beatles, the Stones or anyone else you would care to name—was actually coming to Memphis and six other cities. I was 23 years old, newly married and was by far the oldest person I knew with any interest at all in the band. I subscribed to *Rolling Stone* magazine and was as shocked as everyone else when I read a cover story by Charles M. Young about a new rock and roll movement in England called "punk" that was spearheaded by a spike-haired group of angry working-class misfits called the Sex Pistols. The name alone seemed calculated to outrage the status quo including the staid rock press.

I immediately wanted to check them out.

The *Rolling Stone* article didn't exactly endorse the band or their music, but it was a powerful advertisement for an indefinable something that they were selling in their attitude. I had no idea what to expect when I gave "Pretty Vacant" its first spin, but from its first repeated guitar signature followed by a thunder of drums then the nastiest-sounding power chords this side of the Who's *Live at Leeds* I was completely hooked. My wife, predictably, hated it as did every friend I pigeon-holed into listening to the song. As I say, the music of "Pretty Vacant" could be compared distantly to other rock music I had heard and, indeed, loved such as *Live at Leeds*. But nothing prepared me for the raw, screaming, snarling mess that was the utterly unique voice of Johnny Rotten.

As a teacher, at various times I've tried to explain to my students just how revolutionary the Beatles were when they first appeared in America. I was in the fourth grade and because my parents were strictly-observant Southern Baptists, I never got a chance to watch *The Ed Sullivan Show* (we attended church every Sunday morning and Sunday night). I had no idea that a rock and roll group called the Beatles had even made an appearance on the *Sullivan Show*. However, the next Saturday I was at a friend's house; his sister was watching American Bandstand. The whole show was devoted to the Beatles and when I asked innocently who the Beatles were a whole group of kids turned to look at me and said in unison, "you don't know who the Beatles are?"

Before I left that house I not only knew all the Beatles by name but I was already practicing my sales pitch for getting Mom and Dad to buy me one of their records. The way they looked, their hair, their clothes, their sound, their photos, the graphics on their album covers—nothing about them was familiar ground. It was as if a flying saucer from Planet Cool had deposited four of its subjects on Earth to change all the young people. Elvis was instantly passé.

The Sex Pistols were similar in many ways. Their look was new, their sound different, and they brought with them a whole new aesthetic. Even their album graphics, as mentioned, were revolutionary. They brought danger back to rock and roll and we in Memphis knew they were going to be a force to be reckoned with.

As I recall, the tickets for the concert cost $3.50. I bought three—one for myself, one for my wife, and one for a friend. They still haven't forgiven me. The concert was going to be held in a dilapidated former ballroom (the Taliesyn) attached to the 20th Century Club on Union Avenue. I do not recall any rock concerts being booked there prior to the Sex Pistols. The ballroom supposedly held 900 people, but no one mentioned that this was to be the highly dangerous festival seating, where concertgoers are herded like cattle into an open room and made to stand without seating for hours. Police Director Buddy Chapman, already worried that the Sex Pistols might instigate some sort of riot, along with Fire Marshals, declared the festival seating arrangement unsafe (they were dead right about this) and required the promoter to put seats in the room. In so doing at least 200 people holding tickets—astoundingly, the concert was a sellout—were left outdoors in the freezing cold drizzle and did not take kindly to the notion that they weren't going to be admitted inside. But more on that in a moment.

Being a lifelong Memphian, I knew it was best to show up early to get a good seat. As we arrived I heard the sounds of "Pretty Vacant" shaking the building; the Sex Pistols were inside doing a sound check. Not being able to yet enter from the front, we ran around back to try and catch a glimpse of them. A very small crowd gathered and suddenly there were shouts of "Sid! Sid!" "Johnny! Johnny!" They were hustled out quickly, enough so that only a few people sighted them and they were not to be seen again for several long hours (note: Sid wandered away from his Holiday Inn room to try and score a heroin fix. It took his handlers several hours to find him).

Fast forward: The ballroom was packed, cameras hovered everywhere, and a lot of the crowd obviously were from the media. Only one kid was dressed punkishly—he was the only one who got that memo apparently—and when he half-heartedly threw a piece of ice at some bright camera lights the cameraman WENT OFF and the kid, obviously no street fighter, slunk down in his chair and didn't stir again until the band came out. A warm-up band, Quo Jr., played first, and they got a very nasty and rude reception from a crowd that was totally amped-up for the Pistols. I have never felt such anticipation and electricity in a crowd before or since and it was both exhilarating and very frightening. The feeling was as if we'd been soaked in some inflammable juju and were waiting for the first spark to ignite us. Quo Jr. was a local, all-black punk band led by the charismatic Roland Robinson (now deceased) who at one point screamed "Man, we can't communicate!"

Then he launched into a high-volume song of the same title. However, the crowd was composed mostly of thrill-seekers (by the way, the crowd was entirely white) who seemingly didn't give a damn about the music, especially that of a black warm-up band. All night long the audience threw ice from soft drink cups—the only refreshment for sale—and the cups themselves (note: Years later I had the pleasure of reminiscing with Roland Robinson about that night. He was amazed that I could remember the name of that song).

After Quo Jr. left the stage the wait seemed interminable. I went to the restroom and right above my head a window shattered and a rock tumbled to the floor. The ticket holders outside were nearly rioting and I could hear someone on a bullhorn (Police Director Buddy Chapman) trying to calm the crowd down outdoors. After about an hour and a half with the tension thick enough to slice, the lights dimmed and out strolled the band who quickly fired up the stage. There were no giant video screens and I could lie and say how small they seemed from my seat midway back. But they seemed HUGE. The crowd seemed stunned. At one point Johnny Rotten even said, "Why are you all staring at me?" They had nowhere near the amplification firepower of someone like the Who but MY GOD when Steve Jones and Paul Cook thundered down I thought the Taliesyn Ballroom would fall to pieces. Steve Jones looked as if he had stepped out of Don Pedro's hair salon. He had a sculpted coif that didn't look punk in the least, but his white Les Paul shredded all notions of a fancy boy. Paul Cook, a stunning drummer, rooted the band's sound to his rhythmic, powerful pounding. The t-shirt he wore contained a close-up photo of a woman's bare breasts.

Sid Vicious, none of us knew at the time, could not play bass guitar at all. His sound was so thick and muddy you could not distinguish notes; all you could hear was a huge, earth-swallowing throb.

Sid was shirtless and had red markings all over his torso. I didn't know until much later that he had carved a message into his chest with a knife: "I need a fix." He wore leather pants and his hair was spiked as was Johnny Rotten's. Sid attempted to talk several times between songs but his accent was impenetrable. Something else no one has mentioned previously is that Johnny Rotten's voice was heavily reverbed, so much so that in one particular instance when he began to speak to the crowd all you could hear was echo. He gave a deadly look to someone off-stage who corrected the problem and we could then hear him speak.

What did he say? "I'm not here for your amusement, you're here for mine. So, behave yourselves and don't throw things at me. I don't like it." I seem to also remember some quips about Elvis. Johnny wore a blue tartan suit and in the spotlights his blue eyes blazed like pilot lights on a stove. He mimicked some of the Shakespearean mannerisms of Sir Laurence Olivier, particularly Richard III, hunchbacked, rocking back and forth as he sang dementedly, appearing ape-like at times, deliberately of course. Sid's bass was slung lower than I had ever seen anyone play a musical instrument. At one point a member of the stage crew held a bottle of Heineken for him to drink while he played. He looked like a baby nursing.

Few people in the audience knew any of the songs, as I mentioned. But that didn't stop the crowd from wanting an encore when the Pistols left the stage. I've read that Memphis was one of the few times the band ever gave an encore, in this case "No Fun," a song originally by the Stooges.

My ears rang for days. My wife complained every time I played the Sex Pistols album, which I managed to finally buy a couple of weeks later. "It was history, baby" I kept telling her. She scoffed.

Some weeks later I met a worker for the telephone company, a big Southern bubba-type, who told me he and some friends had been hired as bodyguards for the Sex Pistols. "Yeah," he laughed, "that damn Sid guy. That scrawny little bastard kept wanting to fight everybody." "What did you do?" I asked. "Aw man, we just laughed at him and pushed him away. He wud'n gonna hurt none of us." And you know, I was right. It was history.

THE END OF THE ROAD

The tour was starting to take its toll. Johnny Rotten was suffering from a terrible bout of the flu and coughing up blood. He was disgusted by the behavior of his friend Sid and felt isolated and alienated from Paul Cook and Steve Jones who had a strong friendship. On January 14, 1978, the tour reached its final date at the Winterland Ballroom in San Francisco. At the end of the show, Rotten was looking tired and disillusioned. He introduced the encore, the Stooges' "No Fun," saying, "You'll get one number and one number only, cause I'm a lazy bastard." As he reached the end of the song, he began to chant, "This is No Fun . . . No Fun . . . This is No Fun . . . At all . . . No Fun." At the very end of the song, Rotten stared at the audience and cackled, "ha ha ha . . . ever get the feeling you've been cheated?", then said "good night," threw down the microphone stand, and walked offstage. He later would explain, "I felt cheated, and I wasn't going on with it any longer. It was a ridiculous farce. Sid was completely out of his brains. . . . Just a waste of space. The whole thing was a joke at that point. . . . Malcolm wouldn't speak to me. . . . He would not discuss anything with me. But then he would turn around and tell Paul and Steve that the tension was all my fault" (Lydon and Zimmerman 1995).

Three days later, on January 17, the Sex Pistols split up, and it really was all over. The short, incendiary career of the world's top punk rock band had come to what was, perhaps, an inevitable end. They made their separate ways to Los Angeles. Paul Cook and Steve Jones remained friendly with Malcolm McLaren and the three of them flew to Rio de Janeiro for a vacation. Sid Vicious stayed in Los Angeles and was in such bad shape that he was immediately taken to the hospital. Johnny Rotten was left alone with little money, not even enough to pay for his flight home or a hotel room. He felt deflated and stranded, let down by his bandmates, and disgusted with the behavior of his manager, Malcolm McLaren. Eventually, he managed to gather the funds to fly to New York, where he announced the breakup of the band in a newspaper interview. He then telephoned Richard Branson, the head of Virgin Records, who paid for his flight home, with a stop off in Jamaica, where Branson met him. In Jamaica, Rotten and Branson met up with members of the American new wave band Devo and there was some discussion of Rotten joining them. This, however, never came about and was probably never a serious proposition.

Epilogue

1979 TO THE PRESENT

This final chapter covers the Pistols later activities and their reunion tours. Johnny Rotten reverted to his real name of John Lydon, and formed Public Image Limited, a post-punk band that played experimental music far removed from the classic punk rock of the Sex Pistols. Jones and Cook teamed up with escaped train robber Ronnie Biggs and recorded a new Pistols single. McLaren continued work on a Pistols movie, which was released as *The Great Rock 'n' Roll Swindle* in 1980. On 12 October 1979, Sid Vicious' girlfriend, Nancy Spungen, was found dead in their New York hotel room. Sid was charged with her murder, although he claimed to have no memory of what had occurred. Vicious died of an overdose on 2 February 1979. In 1996, the Sex Pistols original line-up of John Lydon, Glen Matlock, Steve Jones, and Paul Cook reformed for the "Filthy Lucre" world tour, including 70 concerts to more people than the Sex Pistols ever played to originally. This was followed by further reunions in 2002 and 2007.

This epilogue covers the Pistols later activities and some personal recollections of events I attended in recent years including a reunion gig, a book signing and interview with John Lydon, and an interview with Malcolm McLaren. This section concludes by discussing how their legacy has helped shape modern music, fashion, and culture, and discusses how punk has become accepted as part of the establishment. No Sex Pistols, no Nirvana, no Green Day. In 2006, Vivienne Westwood became a Dame. Malcolm McLaren died in 2010; his coffin was sprayed "Too Fast to Live; Too Young to Die." In 2008, John Lydon appeared in a television advertising campaign for Country Life butter, wearing a tweed suit; every inch the country gent.

PUBLIC IMAGE LTD

John Lydon's next move after the Sex Pistols was not what you would have expected from the leading face of punk rock. The band that he formed, Public Image Ltd, was a unique blend of reggae and world music. Their music was in many ways a screaming cacophony of sound and would alienate many of his punk fan base. For the members of Public Image Ltd (PiL), Lydon turned to his old friend Jah Wobble (a.k.a. John Wardle) who he had been to school with and was one of the "Gang of Johns," which also included Sid Vicious. Lydon encouraged Wobble to learn to play bass guitar, as he had done with Vicious. The band needed a guitarist and approached Keith Levene, whom he had met when Keith was a member of the early Clash, when they supported the Pistols at an early gig. The group then advertised for a drummer in Melody Maker and recruited Jim Walker, a Canadian student who had just arrived in the UK. PiL then began rehearsing in May 1978 and released their first single "Public Image" in October 1978. The single was well received and reached number 9 in the UK charts. PiL performed their first gigs at the Rainbow Theatre, London at Christmas 1978. I was lucky enough to see one of their early gigs when they played in Manchester in early 1979.

Creation for Liberation Benefit Gig, Manchester Belle Vue, 23 February 1979

This was Public Image Ltd's 5th gig, and their first in the North of England. The concert was entitled "Creation for Liberation" and was a benefit gig in aid of the "Race Today Friendly Society." Also on the bill were Bristol's The Pop Group (punky/jazzy/art rock), Merger (a great reggae band), and poets Linton Kwesi Johnson and John Cooper Clarke. We arrived early to see all the bands. I remember seeing a lot of people from the Manchester punk scene; a couple of members of The Buzzcocks were in the crowd. Everyone had turned out to see what John's new band was like. I remember both dub poet Linton Kwesi

Johnson ("England Is a Bitch" was a stand-out) and local hero John Cooper Clarke (super-fast punk poetry) going down well, and then there was a long wait for PiL. The line-up of PiL was: John Lydon (vocals), Keith Levene (guitar), Jah Wobble (bass), and Eddie Edwards (from The Vibrators sitting in on drums for this one gig). There was a long, cold, wait before PiL came on stage. When they did, they wandered on and Lydon famously said to the waiting crowd, "No gimmicks, no theatre, just us. Take it or leave it." They then launched into "Theme" and played a set that featured songs from their first album, and the controversial Pistols' songs "Belsen Was a Gas" (this was the last time that PiL would ever perform the song, and the last time that it was performed live until the Pistols played it again during their reunion tour in 2002). The sound was poor and murky and you couldn't hear Lydon's vocals very well at all. John was as scary and engaging as ever, but overall the band's performance was a little shaky, and lacking the power and depth that PiL can achieve on a good night. I was hoping we would get a Pistols' hit for the encore (I should have known that was never going to happen), but they simply played "Annalisa" again. It was great to see Lydon on stage again, and in a strange way, this was a memorable concert. It represented everything that PiL was about at the time: challenging, strange, not quite what you would expect, noisy, and discordant.

Set List: "Theme," "Annalisa," "Low Life," "Religion," "Attack," "Belsen Was a Gas," "Public Image," "Annalisa"

Public Image Ltd, Newcastle Academy, 6 August 2012

At last, I finally "got" what Public Image Ltd are about. This was the first time I've seen Lydon's band for many years. My wife Marie and I went to one of their first live performances at Manchester Belle Vue in 1979. At the time, the difference between PiL and Lydon's previous band, The Sex Pistols, was just too great for me and many people in the audience. I couldn't believe or understand the noise that they were making and actually wondered if they were serious or whether it was some sort of huge joke. I saw them a couple of times after that at gigs at Newcastle City Hall, and although each time I enjoyed the experience, I still remained unconvinced. Until now. I went along on spec, deciding to go to the gig at the last minute. I'd read reviews of recent PiL gigs, which have all been very positive. Now I knew why. The band were just great that night in Newcastle Academy. I arrived just in time for the show, and scored a ticket outside for £20, making a small saving on the £25 face value (result!).

The place was packed full of oldish punky types, and everyone was ready and up for the occasion. There was no support act, and the band came on stage around 8:45 p.m., opening with "This Is Not a Love Song," which set the tone for the night. Loud, throbbing beats, Lydon's impassioned vocals, and jangling, discordant guitars. The band were so together and so very tight. Every song was epic, and Lydon sang his heart out. At one point, he told us "I'm like a fine wine, I mature with age" and he wasn't far wrong. His voice was amazing and so strong. Last time I saw him was fronting the reformed Sex Pistols at Brixton Academy, and although that was a great gig, at times Lydon seemed to be treating it all as a bit of fun. Not last night, he was deadly serious as he spat out the vocals, leered at us, and told us "Friends are for forgiving, Politicians are for killing." Very dark, very intense, very passionate, and much, much better than I imagined or could have hoped for. Some bands can reinvent themselves and come back even better.

THE RONNIE BIGGS INCIDENT

One of the next adventures for the Sex Pistols was quite bizarre, to say the least. After the band split, Steve Jones and Paul Cook flew to Brazil where they met up with escaped train robber Ronnie Biggs. Biggs had been part of the gang that took part in the infamous Great Train Robbery in the UK in the 1960s. The great train robbery was a robbery of £2.6 million from a Royal mail train that was traveling from Glasgow to London in the early hours of 8 August 1963. Ronnie Biggs was a member of the 15-strong gang who robbed the train (Gosling, Dennis, and Craig 1964). Biggs was imprisoned in 1965, but soon escaped and fled to Australia and then Rio de Janeiro, Brazil. The liaison with the Sex Pistols was a publicity stunt for both the band and Ronnie Biggs himself. Biggs recorded two songs with Jones and Cook and these were released as a single in the UK. They also appeared on the soundtrack of *The Great Rock 'n' Roll Swindle* film. The first track was "No One Is Innocent (The Biggest Blow: A Punk Prayer/Cosh the Driver)." The song was (deliberately) in bad taste and designed to shock, presumably at the instigation of Malcolm McLaren. The single's sleeve featured an actor dressed as Nazi leader Martin Bormann playing bass with the group. The second song recorded with Ronnie Biggs was a version of the Pistols' "Belsen Was a Gas." The liaison with Biggs was short and not the greatest part of the Pistols' career.

THE GREAT ROCK 'N' ROLL SWINDLE

Malcolm McLaren had been planning for a film based around the Pistols for some time. In the end, the soundtrack album for *The Great Rock 'n' Roll Swindle* film was completed before the movie. The soundtrack album was released by Virgin Records in February 1979. It consisted mostly of tracks credited to the Sex Pistols; however, these were new recordings without Johnny Rotten as singer. The singers were, in fact, Steve Jones, Sid Vicious, Paul Cook, Ronnie Biggs (as discussed above), and Tenpole Tudor, who was also considered as a replacement vocalist for Johnny Rotten. Even Malcolm McLaren takes the vocals on a couple of tracks. Some tracks feature Johnny Rotten's vocals from unused recordings. There is one live cut from the band's final concert in San Francisco.

Despite the strange nature of the recordings, the album resulted in four top 10 singles in the UK. These were "No One Is Innocent" (featuring Ronnie Biggs), Sid Vicious' cover of the Eddie Cochran song "Something Else," Steve Jones singing a new song "Silly Thing," and Sid Vicious' cover of Eddie Cochran's "C'mon Everybody."

The film, *The Great Rock 'n' Roll Swindle*, was finally released in 1980 having been directed by Julien Temple. The movie is based on McLaren's view of the band and the rise of punk rock. McLaren tells a story of how he created the band and the entire punk rock movement, which was "an invention of mine they called the punk rock" (Temple, 1982). Temple believed that the Pistols had become the "poster on the bedroom wall of the day where you kneel down last thing at night and pray to your rock god. And that was never the point. . . . The myth had to be dynamited in some way. We had to make this film in a way to enrage the fans" (Salewicz 2001).

THE DEATH OF SID VICIOUS

After the Sex Pistols split up, Sid Vicious moved to New York and started performing as a solo artist. Sid's girlfriend, Nancy Spungen, began acting as his manager. His first new activity as a solo artist was to record a new album, *Sid Sings*, which was to be released later in 1979. The album was recorded live and he was backed by a band known as The Idols, who included Arthur Kane and Jerry Nolan from the New York Dolls. However, tragedy was soon to strike.

Sid and Nancy moved into the Chelsea Hotel, a famous haunt for numerous writers, musicians, and artists. Over the years, the Chelsea Hotel had been home to famous artists such as Dylan Thomas, Alan Ginsberg, Leonard Cohen, Janis Joplin, and Jim Morrison. On 12 October 1978, Nancy Spungen was found dead in the hotel. She was in the room that she shared with Sid, and was found with stab wounds to her stomach. She was surrounded by paraphernalia connected with drug use and the police soon arrested Sid Vicious and charged him with her murder. There was much suspicion and unanswered questions around the death of Nancy, some of which suggested she may have been murdered by a drug dealer, rather than by Sid. Others believed that Nancy had committed suicide. McLaren said at the time "I can't believe he was involved in such a thing. Sid was set to marry Nancy in New York. He was very close to her and had quite a passionate affair with her" (BBC 1978). Sid was granted bail; however, he was soon to be in trouble again. In an altercation with Patti Smith's brother Todd Smith, he pushed a beer mug into Todd's face and was rearrested and charged with assault. He was soon sent to the notorious Rikers Island Jail, in which he was incarcerated for almost two months. While in jail, Sid was forced to undertake a detoxification program for his drug use. He was released from jail on 1 February 1979 and immediately organised a party to celebrate his release. Sometime during that party, Sid Vicious died of a heroin overdose. His body was discovered by his mother. He was just 21 years old.

Lydon said, "Poor Sid. The only way he could live up to what he wanted everyone to believe about him was to die. That was tragic, but more for Sid than anyone else. He really bought his public image" (Gilmore 1980). Sid had said in 1977 "I'll probably die by the time I reach 25. But I'll have lived the way I wanted to" (Vermorel and Vermorel 1987).

REUNIONS

In 1996, much to the surprise of fans and the music press, the original four Sex Pistols reunited for a six-month tour entitled the Filthy Lucre Tour. The tour included dates across Europe, the USA, Australia, and Japan. In 2002, the band reunited again to celebrate the Queen's Golden Jubilee in their own style, playing a concert at Crystal Palace, London. The next year, in 2003, their Piss off Tour covered the USA for three weeks. In 2007, the Sex Pistols reunited yet again for a short tour of the UK. I was lucky enough to attend one of these shows at Brixton Academy, London. The band continued to play, taking their Combine Harvester Tour across Europe.

Sex Pistols, Brixton Academy, London, 10 November 2007

John Lydon: "It started out as one night at Brixton . . . We thought maybe 5,000 will want to see us, but it's turned into a bigger monster than any of us had any concept of." In fact, the Sex Pistols ended up playing to 60,000 fans during their brief 2007 reunion tour, camping for five nights at Brixton Academy and then adding two massive arena shows in Manchester and Glasgow.

I've already written about the two occasions in which I was lucky enough to see The Sex Pistols in their prime, once in 1976 and once in 1977. I passed on their 1996 Filthy Lucre and 2002 Golden Jubilee reunion gigs. I figured it was never going to be the same. Well, of course, it wasn't going to be the same, but it could still be bloody great! When I saw that they were reuniting again in 2007 for a few dates at Brixton, I relented and bought tickets. The dates were to mark the 30th anniversary of the release of the band's seminal album *Never Mind the Bollocks*.

David (my son) and I arrived early for the gig, and watched support band The Cribs, who seemed very much out of the punk mould. By the time the Pistols were due on stage, the place was completely ram packed, almost dangerously so. The audience was, as you would expect, largely aging punks; lots of Mohican haircuts and studded leather jackets. Before the Pistols came on stage, the hall was filled with the sound of Vera Lynn's "There's Always Be an England," which prompted mass singalong (and sadly quite a few right-arm salutes). I'm not sure it was the most appropriate song to open the concert with, but it certainly got the crowd going. The band walked on stage Rotten as wide-eyed as ever.

They hurled themselves into "Pretty Vacant" and the place went completely bananas. An atmosphere, a band, a crowd, and a punk anthem like no other. There never was, never has been, and never will be anyone who can touch these guys. Rotten was sneering, his snarling vocal as thrilling and powerful as ever. Flanked, as in 1976, by Steve Jones, ever the guitar hero, and Glen Matlock looking ever the cool guy.

All the hits and most of the *Bollocks* album are played; an immense crashing version of "Holidays in the Sun" with Paul Cock slamming the drums, Rotten spitting out the lyrics to The Stooge's "No Fun," and a backdrop of our safety-pin-sporting queen is lowered behind them for "God Save the Queen." Halfway through the set, David and I make our way toward the back of the hall, it's just too full and too hot down near the front. Then there is the inevitable encore of "Anarchy in the U.K.," at which point I swear every single person in the venue is singing at the top of their voice. They return again to play a cover of Jonathan Richman's "Roadrunner." We walked out in the cold London air, stunned; knowing that we had experienced something special.

Well, of course, no, it wasn't the same. We were older and so were the Pistols. The crowd was bigger than those they played to in their heyday (when I saw them in 1976 there were 50 to 100 people there, a few hundred in 1977). We knew all the songs this time. But these old guys could still sneer at society and play some of the best rock 'n' roll produced by any band. Amazing. Scary. Stunning. I have the DVD and play it every now and then to remind myself of that night.

Setlist: "Pretty Vacant," "Seventeen," "No Feelings," "New York," "Did You No Wrong," "Liar," "Holidays in the Sun," "Submission," "(I'm Not Your) Steppin' Stone," "No Fun," "Problems," "God Save the Queen," "E.M.I."

Encore 1: "Bodies," "Anarchy in the U.K."

Encore 2: "Roadrunner" (Jonathan Richman cover)

Malcolm McLaren, The Baltic, Newcastle, 13 November 2009

Malcolm McLaren continued to make music and talk about his contribution to punk rock. I was lucky enough to go and see him speak at The Baltic Art Gallery in Newcastle in 2009. I was steeped in rock music throughout the early days of punk, and caught all of the major punk gigs in the North East: The Pistols, The Clash, The Damned, The Jam, Vibrators, 999, Siouxsie, Ramones, Television, Iggy, Buzzcocks, and too many others to mention. So, when I saw that Malcolm McLaren was coming to the Baltic Art Gallery to present his new film and talk about his work, I couldn't resist getting tickets to go along and hear what he had to say. I was hoping for some insights into those great days, which are fast becoming fading memories. So, Laura, David (my daughter and son), and I went to this event to hear what Malcolm had to say.

The evening had been sold out for some time and was held in the exhibition space in the Baltic, which holds around 300 people (I would guess). The main part of the evening was the first showing of Malcolm's new film: *Paris*. *Paris* is in 21 sections; each section is a collage of old French commercials overlaid with McLaren speaking, singing, and other music. After the film, Malcolm was interviewed and then he took questions from the audience. Malcolm talked about the film and gave some insights into his contribution to punk. This was, as always, Malcolm's view that he invented the Pistols and the punk genre.

Malcolm McLaren died in 2010; his coffin was sprayed "Too Fast to Live; Too Young to Die."

"We were all warriors together," John Lydon, Manchester, 9 October 2014

The launch event for his new autobiography: *Anger Is an Energy: My Life Uncensored*. From the publicity for the event: "John Lydon will be taking part in an exclusive no-holds-barred live onstage interview with DJ/writer Dave Haslam, discussing his turbulent life, from his beginnings as a sickly child of immigrant Irish parents who grew up in post-war London to his present status as an alternative national hero, via the Sex Pistols, Public Image Ltd (PiL), collaborations with Afrika Bambaataa and Leftfield, compelling opinions, and celebrated TV appearances.

He'll also be signing copies of his autobiography. This will surely be one of Manchester's most memorable pop culture events of the year."

About the venue (from the website): "A Grade II listed Wesleyan chapel in Manchester City Centre closed and hidden for over 40 years. Resurrected by Trof, the people behind Gorilla and The Deaf Institute, as an unrivalled events venue, restaurant and bar. The grand and ornate chapel has been restored into a stunning purpose-built music hall and is set to become one of the most atmospheric music and events venues in the UK."

I arrived in Manchester early, around 6 p.m., had a coffee and then joined the queue for entry to the Albert Hall. I took a seat in the front row, and waited for the great man to arrive. Shortly after the advertised start time of 7:30 p.m., DJ Dave Haslam walked on stage, and introduced John Lydon, who received a standing ovation from the crowd. For the next hour or so, Dave and John discussed John's life. Lydon was as controversial and opinionated as you might expect, giving us his views on politics and how all the parties have moved toward the same ground, his early life and poor health and his respect for the NHS, his relationship with Sid Vicious, that Sid was named after his mum's hamster and was a fan of singer Leo Sayer. And how he stills misses him, his belief in the working class and family values, and some thoughts on the birth of punk and how it was needed at the time, and is needed again. The man wears his soul on his sleeve, and in strongly protective of the punk values that he obviously holds so dear. The audience clearly loved him, showing this by giving him several standing ovations. After an hour or so, Dave opened up questions to the floor, and gave members of the audience a chance to throw questions at John, via a roving mike. One guy asked his favourite gigs; he quoted a recent appearance at Manchester and at a massive festival in Croatia; another complemented his music tastes, which are wide-ranging and include The Kinks and Van Der Graaf Generator. After another thirty minutes or so, the first part of the evening concluded and we all went downstairs to the basement where John was doing the book signing. It was 9 p.m.

I rushed downstairs as quickly as I could, but by the time I got there, the queue was already large. I reckon I ended up about half way back in the queue, which swirled around and around the basement, controlled by rows of barriers. Reggae music was blasting as we waited in anticipation for our individual audience with Johnny Rotten, all nervously clutching our books. To his credit, John took his time to talk to everyone while signing, spending a few minutes with each person, and there were two or three hundred waiting. Because of this, movement was slow and it seemed to take forever to get to the front. In fact, it took me more than three hours to get to meet John Lydon. I had a quick chat with him, and asked him if he remembered the first Pistols gig that I witnessed in Whitby in 1976. I foolishly mentioned that the "Pistols were thrown off stage." John looked me straight in the eye and said "What did you say? Nobody ever threw me off any stage." I quickly corrected my statement and made it clear that what actually happened was that the DJ turned the sound off. "Ah . . . Now that's different" said John, smiling. It was after 12:30 a.m. when I left the venue. Got home at 3:15 a.m. Tired this morning, but glad I went; it was a fascinating evening spent with a true legend and "one off." Everyone there had so many warm feelings and so much respect for the guy; a man who continues to "always tell it as it is." Lydon is an enigma; challenging, frustrating, rude, fearless, authentic, insightful; all of those things and more.

LEGACY

The legacy of punk and the Sex Pistols is undeniable. They have influenced hundreds of bands and punk fashion continues to reappear in many different forms. Without the Sex Pistols, there would be no U2, no Nirvana, no Green Day. The impact of the band and their album *Never Mind the Bollocks* continues to this day.

This book has covered the history of the band and some of my own personal recollections of a rock band the likes of which we will never see again.

FURTHER READING

Web Resources

The official Sex Pistols site:
   http://www.philjens.plus.com/pistols/pistols/links.html
The official John Lydon site:
   http://www.johnlydon.com/
The official Public Image Limited site:
   http://www.pilofficial.com/info.html
The official Steve Jones site:
   http://www.jonesysjukebox.com/
The official Glen Matlock site:
   http://www.glenmatlock.co.uk/

FURTHER LISTENING

Album

1977 *Never Mind the Bollocks, Here's the Sex Pistols*: UK chart position No. 1

Bootleg album

1977 *Spunk* (early recordings of debut album)

Film Soundtrack

1979 *The Great Rock 'n' Roll Swindle*: UK chart position No. 7

Singles

Year	Single	UK Singles Chart Position
1976	"Anarchy in the U.K."	38
1976	"God Save the Queen"	2
1977	"Pretty Vacant"	6
1977	"Holidays in the Sun"	8
1978	"No One Is Innocent/My Way"	7
1978	"Something Else/Frigging in the Rigging"	3
1978	"Silly Thing/Who Killed Bambi?"	6
1979	"C'Mon Everybody"	3
1979	"The Great Rock 'n' Roll Swindle"	21

REFERENCES

Adams, Ruth. 2008. "The Englishness of English Punk: Sex Pistols, Subcultures, and Nostalgia." *Popular Music and Society* 31: 469–88.

Albiez, Sean. 2005. "Print the Truth, Not the Legend: Sex Pistols, Lesser Free Trade Hall, Manchester, 4 June 1976." In *Performance and Popular Music: History, Place and Time*, edited by Ian Inglis, 92–106. Abingdon: Ashgate Publishing.

Anger, K. 1963. *Scorpio Rising.* Puck Film Productions.

Back, L. 2002. "God Save the Queen: The Pistols' Jubilee." *Open Democracy*, 31 May.

BBC News. 1977. "EMI Fires Sex Pistols," BBC, 6 January.

———. 1978. "Sex Pistol Vicious on Murder Charge," BBC.

Belfast Telegraph. 2013. "Interview with Glen Matlock."

Bendel, G. 2015. "From punk to postman with Vic Godard." *Huck*, https://www.huckmag.com/art-and-culture/film-2/subway-sect-graham-bendel/.

Billboard. 1977. Review of *Never Mind the Bollocks, Here's the Sex Pistols*.

Black, J. 1996. "Review of Sex Pistols in Manchester." *Mojo*. December.

bombedoutpunk website, http://www.bombedoutpunk.com/ (accessed 22 July 2018).

Branson, R. 1998. *Losing My Virginity*. Sydney, Australia: Random House.

Bromberg, C. 1989. *The Wicked Ways of Malcolm McLaren*. London: Omnibus Press.

Burchill, J., and Parsons, T. 1987. *The Boy Looked at Johnny: The Obituary of Rock and Roll*. London: Faber & Faber.

Burridge, A. 2008. Review of *Spunk* on *Amazon*.

Butcher, J. 2012. "North Punks Harry Hack and The Big G to Release Debut CD of '70s Demos." *Evening Chronicle*, November.

Calef, S. 2009. "Physical Graffiti." In *Led Zeppelin and Philosophy*. Illinois: Open Court.

Cash, J. 1968. *At Folsom Prison*. Columbia Records.

Chua, L. 2000. "Artists in Conversation: Julien Temple." *Bomb*, 72.

Clinton, H. 2003. *Bootleg: The Rise & Fall of the Secret Recording Industry.* London: Omnibus Press.

Cobley, P. 1999. "Leave the Capitol." In *Punk Rock: So What? The Cultural Legacy of Punk*, edited by Roger Sabin, 170–85. London: Routledge.

Collins, T. 1976. report in *New Musical Express*.

Coon, C. 1976a. "Punk on Stage." *Melody Maker*, December.

———. 1976b. "The Clash: Down and Out and Proud." *Melody Maker*, November.

———. 1976c. "The Sex Pistols: Club De Chalet Du Lac, Paris." *Melody Maker*, September.

———. 1982. *1988: The New Wave Punk Rock Explosion*. London: Omnibus Press.

Coupland, N., 2011. "Voice, Place, and Genre in Popular Song Performance." *Journal of Sociolinguistics*, 15(5), 573–602.

Coventry Telegraph. 2013. "The Giants of Punk Rock the Lanch Bar." 26 April.
Crabtree, S. (director) 2004. *Blood on the Turntable: The Sex Pistols*. BBC documentary.
Crossley, N. 2009. "The Man Whose Web Expanded: Network Dynamics in Manchester's Post/Punk Music Scene 1976–1980." *Poetics*, 37(1): 24–49.
Dadamo, G. 1976. "The A–Z of Punk," *Sounds*.
———. 1977. "Sex Pistols: 'Jooh-Nee! Jooh-Nee! Jooh-Nee!'" *Sounds*, August.
Dahlin, T. 2012. *A Vicious love story*. UK: New Haven Publishing.
Daily Mirror. 1976. "The Filth and the Fury." December.
Daily Mirror. 1977. "Report of the Sex Pistols at Heathrow Airport," July.
Dalton, D. 1997. *El Sid*. New York: St. Martin's Press.
Davies, J. 1996. "The Future of 'No Future': Punk Rock and Postmodern Theory." *Journal of Popular Culture* 29(4): 3–25.
Debord, G. 2012. *The Society of the Spectacle*. New York: Bread and Circuses.
Deriso, N. 2014. "'Some of it was a little bit overblown': Jethro Tull's Ian Anderson on prog rock's ups and downs," http://somethingelsereviews.com.
Delplanque, P. "Rock Garden Recollections." *Middlesbrough Gazette*, September 2010.
Double O. 2007. "Punk Rock as Popular Theatre." *New Theatre Quarterly* 23(1): 35–48.
Egan, S. 2014. *The Clash: The Only Band That Mattered*. Lanham, MD: Rowman & Littlefield.
EMI. 1976. Press release. 7 December.
Enough Rope with Andrew Denton [TV programme]. 2006. CrackerJack Productions, Australia.
Farber, J. 1977. "Rick Denies Press Rumours in Sex Pistols Controversy." *Circus*.
Fear, D. 2015. "Julien Temple on 'Lost' Pistols Film, Punk Docs & Joe Strummer's Socks." *Rolling Stone*, 30 July.
Fitzsimons, R. 2013. *I'm an Upstart: The Decca Wade Story*. London: Ardra Press.
Foxx, J. 2008. "The Quiet Man Speaks." *The Quietus*, 7 November.
Garnett, Rt. 1999. "Too Low to Be Low: Art Pop and the Sex Pistols." In *Punk Rock: So What? The Cultural Legacy of Punk*, edited by Roger Sabin. London: Routledge.
Gilmore, M. 1980. "John Lydon Improves His Public Image," *Rolling Stone*.
Gimarc, G. 2006. *Punk Diary: Ultimate Trainspotter's Guide to Underground Rock, 1970–1982*. San Francisco: Backbeat Books.
Gosling, G., Dennis, B., and Craig, J. 1964. *The Great Train Robbery*. London: Allen.
Green, J., and Barker, G., 1999. *A Riot of Our Own: Night and Day with The Clash*. London: Macmillan.
Greig, S., McCarthy, M., and Peacock, J. 1976. "The Filth and the Fury," *Daily Mirror*, 2 December.
Griffiths, J. 2017. "Just the Ticket: Richard Branson pays for 'B°°°°es on Tour' hen Party to Go on 'Dream Holiday' to Las Vegas." *The Sun*, 4 June.
Gunn, J. 1999. "Gothic Music and the Inevitability of Genre." *Popular Music & Society* 23(1): 31–50.
Hamblett, C., and Deverson, J. 1964. *Generation X*. London: Tandem.
Hasham, D. 2015. *Life after Dark: A History of British Nightclubs & Music Venues*. New York: Simon & Schuster.
Hedley, O. 1977. *The Queen's Silver Jubilee: A Pictorial Souvenir*. London: Pitkin.
Henry, S. 2008. "Atlanta Punk! A Reunion for 688 and Metroplex." *Creative Loafing*, October.
Heylin, C. 2000. *Never Mind the Bollocks, Here's the Sex Pistols*. New York: Schirmer Trade Books.
Hodgkinson, W. 2006. *Guitar Man*. Boston: Da Capo Press.
Hoffman, P. 1989. *Violence in Modern Philosophy*. Chicago: University of Chicago Press.
Hook, P. 2012. *Unknown Pleasures: Inside Joy Division*. London: Simon & Schuster.
Hornby, N. 2007. Foreword in *Great Interviews of the 20th Century: Sex Pistols, Bill Grundy 1976, The Guardian*.
Houghton, M. 1975. "So What is Punk Rock?," *Let It Rock*. December.
Hoye, J. 2003. *VH1's 100 Greatest Albums*. London: Pocket Books.

Hume, M. 2012. "It's Not 1977 All Over Again." *Spiked*, June.

Hynde, C. 2015. *Reckless: My Life as a Pretender*. London: Ebury.

The Independent. 2006. "Never Mind Four-Letter Words . . . Here's the Sex Pistols: When Television Met Punk Rock." December 1.

Ingham, J. 1976. "Report of Sex Pistols at Manchester Free Trade Hall." *Sounds*, 31 July.

———. 1976. The Sex Pistols are 4 months old . . ., *Sounds*.

Jones, S. 2018. in http://www.herestheartwork.co.uk (accessed 16 July 2018).

Joynson, V. 2001. *Up Yours! A Guide to UK Punk, New Wave & Early Post Punk*. Wolverhampton: Borderline Publications.

Kane, A. K. 2009. *I, Doll: Life and Death with the New York Dolls*. Chicago: Chicago Review Press.

Kelly, I. and Westwood, V. 2014. *Vivienne Westwood*. London: Picador.

Kent, N. 1973. "Review of David Bowie Concert at Earls Court." *New Musical Express*, May.

———. 1976a. "Malcolm McLaren: Meet the Colonel Tom Parker of the Blank Generation." *New Musical Express*, November.

Kent, N. 1976b. "New York: Plug in to the Nerve-ends of the Naked City." *New Musical Express*, March.

———. 1977. "Never Mind the Sex Pistols, Here Comes the Wrath of Sid!" *New Musical Express*, December.

Knewstub, N. 2009. "EMI Guns Down the Sex Pistols," *The Guardian*, 7 January.

Laing, D. 2015. *One Chord Wonders: Power and Meaning in Punk Rock*. Oakland: PM Press.

Langton, C. G. 1990. "Computation at the Edge of Chaos: Phase Transitions and Emergent Computation." *Physica D: Nonlinear Phenomena*, 42(1): 12–37.

Licht, A. 2005. "Art School of Rock." *Modern Painters*, January: 94–97.

Liverpool Echo. 1976. "Call for Boycott on Sex Pistols," 7 December.

London Evening Standard. 1977. "Police Move in on Punk Disc Shops," 9 November.

Long, P. 2006. "The Primary Code: The Meanings of John Peel." *Radio Journal: International Studies in Broadcast and Audio Media* 4(1): 25–48.

Lowry, R., & Myers, B. 2008. *The Clash: Rock Retrospectives*. Coda: Henley.

Lydon, J. 2018. http://www.herestheartwork.co.uk (accessed 16 July 2018).

Lydon, J. 1996. Interview, *Q Magazine*.

Lydon, J., and Zimmerman, K. 1995. *Rotten: No Irish, No Blacks, No Dogs*. New York: Picador.

Marsh, D. 1972. "Detroit." *Creem*.

———. 1973. "Blue Oyster Cult, Wayne County & The Electric Chairs, Kiss, Elliott Murphy, New York Dolls, Teenage Lust & the Lustettes: Various: New York New Wave." *Melody Maker*, 6 October.

Matlock, Glen. 2012. *I Was a Teenage Sex Pistol*. London: Rocket88.

McKenna, K. 2005. Q&A with Steve Jones, *Rhino*.

McLaren, M. 2007. Afterword. *Great Interviews of the 20th Century: Sex Pistols, Bill Grundy 1976. The Guardian* (London), 13–15.

———. 2007 "Searching for a Way to Break the Rules," *The Guardian*, 15 September.

McNeil, L., and McCain, G. 1996. *Please Kill Me: The Uncensored Oral History of Punk*. London: Abacus.

McNeill, P. 1977. "Spitting in the Eye of the Hurricane." *New Musical Express*, January.

Medhurst, A. 1999. "What Did I Get? Punk, Memory and Autobiography." In *Punk Rock: So What? The Cultural Legacy of Punk*, edited by Roger Sabin, 219–31. London: Routledge.

Melody Maker. 1976. "Sex Pistols Sign to EMI."

Melody Maker. 1977. "Pistols Rolling Anarchy Review." 20 August.

Mojo. 2008. "The Sex Pistols." July.

Monk, N., & Gutterman, J. 1990. *12 Days on the Road with the Sex Pistols and America*. New York: Harper.

Moon, T. 2008. *1,000 Recordings to Hear Before You Die*. New York: Workman.

Moran, J. 2013. "Television's Magic Moments." *The Guardian*, 16 August.

Morley, P. 2006. "The Northern Soul." *The Guardian*, 21 May.

Morrisey, S. 1976. Letter to *Melody Maker*, 11 December.

Morrissey. 2013. *Autobiography*. London: Penguin Classics.

Murison, K. 2015. "Golden Hynde." *Sunday Times Magazine*. 30 August, 12.

Murphy, S. 2002. Sleeve notes for *Sexbox*, Virgin Records.

Needs, K. 1977. Review of *Never Mind the Bollocks, Here's the Sex Pistols*. *Zigzag*, November.

Neill, A. and Kent, M. 2007. *Anyway, Anyhow, Anywhere: The Complete Chronicle of The Who 1958–1978*. London: Virgin.

Nissim, M. 2010. "John Lydon: F°°k Malcolm McLaren." *Digital Spy*, 19 July.

Nolan, D. 2006. *I Swear I Was There: The Gig That Changed the World*. London: Independent Music Press.

Odell, M. 2005. "I Want to Take the Sex Pistols to Iraq." *Q*, December.

Patterson, S. 2007. "Never Mind the Sex Pistols, Here's to 30 Years of Bollocks." *Glasgow Herald*. 26 October.

Perry, M. 1976. "Sex Pistols—Any Club, Any Date." *Sniffin' Glue 3*.

———. 1996. *And God Created Punk*. London: Virgin Books.

———. 2009. *Sniffin' Glue and Other Rock 'n' Roll Habits: The Essential Punk Accessory*. London: Omnibus Press.

Poulsen, H. B. 2005. *'77: The Year of Punk and New Wave*. London: Helter Skelter.

Rachel, D. 2014. *The Art of Noise: Conversations with Great Songwriters*. London: Macmillan.

Redstar73. 23 June 2006.

Billboard, Review of *Never Mind the Bollocks, Here's the Sex Pistols*. 1977.

Robb, J., and Fredrickson, L. 2012. *Punk Rock: An Oral History*. Oakland, CA: PM Press.

Robins, W. 1976. "Punk Rock: Its Day Will Come." *Newsweek*, 25 January.

Rock Compact Disc Magazine, Nightingale, W. Interview, 1993.

Rolling Stone, "500 Greatest Songs of All Time," 2004.

Sabin, R. 1999. *Punk Rock: So What? The Cultural Legacy of Punk*. London: Routledge.

Salewicz, C. 2001. "Interview with Julien Temple by Chris Salewicz," *The Great Rock 'n' Roll Swindle*, DVD bonus feature. London: Virgin Video.

Savage, J. 1977a. Review of *Never Mind the Bollocks, Here's the Sex Pistols*. *Sounds*, 5 November.

———. 1977b. "The Sex Pistols: The Screen on the Green, London." *Sounds*, 9 April.

———. 1977c. "What Did You Do on the Jubilee? The Pistols on the Thames." *Sounds*, 18 June.

———. 1991. *England's Dreaming: Sex Pistols and Punk Rock*. London: Faber and Faber.

———. 2005. *England's Dreaming*. London: Faber & Faber.

Scherman, T. "Elvis Dies." 2006. *American Heritage*, 16 August.

Sex Pistols official website, http://www.sexpistolsofficial.com/records/anarchy-in-the-uk-7/ (accessed 21 July 2018).

Shaar Murray, C. 1976. "The Sex Pistols, The Clash, The Buzzcocks: Screen on the Green." *New Musical Express*, 11 September.

Silverton, P. 1976. "Pistols, Clash etc.: What Did You Do on the Punk Tour, Daddy?" *Sounds*, 18 December.

Sloboda, N. 2011. "Something Rotten: The Punk Rock Richard III of Julien Temple's *The Filth and the Fury*." *Literature Film Quarterly* 39(2): 141–50.

Smith, P. 2013. "Ladies and Gentlemen: The Rolling Stones in Concert." In *The Rolling Stones: Sociological Perspectives*, edited by Helmet Staubmann, 201–22. Lanham, MD: Lexington Books.

———. "Holidays in the Sun: The Sex Pistols at the Seaside." *Popular Music and Society* 38(4): 1–13.

———. 2015b. "Holidays in the Sun: The Sex Pistols at the Seaside." *Popular Music and Society* 38(4): 487–99.

———. 2015c. "A Personal History of UK Arena Concerts: Reflections on Gigs over the Past Forty Years." *Arena Rock*.

————. 2017. "An Analysis of the Clash in Concert: 1977 to 1982." In Cohen, S. and Peacock, J. (eds.), *The Clash Takes on the World: Transnational Perspectives on the Only Band That Matters.* London: Bloomsbury.

Southall, B. 2007. *Sex Pistols: 90 Days at EMI.* London: Bobcat Books.

South Wales Echo, 1976. Letter to the *Echo*.

Spencer, N. 1976. "Don't Look over Your Shoulder, the Sex Pistols Are Coming." *New Musical Express*. London.

————. 2012. "1977: The Queen's Punk Jubilee." *The Guardian*, 29 April.

Stephen, A. "Report on Green Goddess," *Sunday Telegraph*, 1977.

Strongman, P. 2008 *Pretty Vacant: A History of UK Punk.* Chicago: Chicago Review Press.

Strummer, J. 2000. "Interview with Joe Strummer." *Record Collector.*

Sumner, B. 2014. *Chapter and Verse [New Order, Joy Division, and Me].* London: Bantam.

Sutcliffe, P. 1978. "Angelic Upstarts: Bolingbroke Hall, South Shields." *Sounds*, 4 March.

————. 1979. "Penetration/Punishment of Luxury/Neon: City Hall, Newcastle." *Sounds*, 6 January.

Sweeney, K. 2012. Interview with Tony Parsons, *The Guardian*, 29 April.

Temple, J. 1982. *The Great Rock 'n' Roll Swindle*. London: Virgin Video.

Temple, J. 2000. *The Filth and the Fury: A Sex Pistols Film*, Film 4 Video.

Terry. 1976. "Pistols in Prison." *Castrated Fanzine* No. 1, September 19. http://chelmsford-rocks.com/sexpistolschelmsford.html (accessed 28 July 2018).

Tobler, J. 1992. *NME Rock 'n' Roll Years*. London, UK: Reed International Books Ltd.

totheleftofwest.livejournal.com (accessed 19 July 2018).

Tse-Tung, M. and Zedong, M. 1961. *On Guerrilla Warfare*. Champaign, IL: University of Illinois Press.

Uncut. 2007. Interview with Paul Weller, August.

Van Ham, L. 2009. "Reading Early Punk as Secularized Sacred Clowning." *Journal of Popular Culture* 42(2): 318–39.

Vermorel, F., and Vermorel, J. 1987. *Sex Pistols: The Inside Story*. London: Undercover.

Ward, E. O. 1969. The Stooges Review, *Rolling Stone*, 18 October.

Watts, R. 2006. Interview with *Punk 77*, November.

Webb, P. and Lynch, J. 2010. "Utopian Punk": The Concept of the Utopian in the Creative Practice of Björk." *Utopian Studies* 21.2: 313–30.

Westwood, V. 2018. "Biography." https://www.businessoffashion.com/community/people/vivienne-westwood.

Westwood, V., and Kelly, I. 2014. *Vivienne Westwood*. London: Picador.

Wolfe, T. 1976. "The Me Decade." *New York*, 23 August.

Wood, L. 1988. *The Sex Pistols Diary: Sex Pistols Day by Day*. London: Omnibus Press.

Zagat. 2003. *1,000 Top Albums of All Time:* New York: Zagat.

Online References

BBC. 2011. "The Sex Pistols in Caerphilly." http://www.bbc.co.uk/wales/music/sites/history/pages/sex-pistols-caerphilly.shtml (accessed 28 July 2018).

BBC, The Watershed. www.bbc.co.uk/worldservice/specials/1738_respect/page9.shtml (accessed 1 April 2017).

Bombedoutpunk. www .bombedoutpunk.com/history/photos-an-account-of-the-sex-pistols-anarchy-tour-in-1976 (accessed 6 May 2017).

Burridge, A. 2008. Review on Amazon. www.amazon.co.uk/Spunk-Sex-Pistols/dp/B000FUU2MQ (accessed 19 June 2017).

Cramp, N. 2006. "The Pistols Are Born: It Happened Here." *Timeout London*. http://www.timeout.com/london/music/the-pistols-are-born-it-happened-here (accessed 28 July 2018).

Fletcher, T. Book Fletcher, T. "Book review of Sniffin' Glue" *iJamming*!, 23 October 2001. https://www.ijamming.net/Music/SniffinGluebook.html (accessed 28 July 2018).

Foster, S. 2012. Peter Smith Personal Blog of Rock Concerts Attended. https://vintage-rock.wordpress.com/2012/07/15/the-clash-white-riot-tour-newcastle-university-may-20th-1977/ (accessed 15 November 2015).

Gallagher, P. 2013. "How the Sex Pistols Saved Christmas," *Dangerous Minds*, http://dangerousminds.net/comments/how_the_sex_pistols_saved_christmas (accessed 25 September 2017).

Geant-Vert. 2009. "The Châlet du Lac Paris 3d and 5th September 1975: The True Story-Eyewitness Accounts," *God Save the Sex Pistols*. http://www.philjens.plus.com/pistols/pistols/ChaletduLac_feature.htm (accessed 28 July 2018).

Harrison, P. 2013. Never Mind the Baubles: Christmas '77 with the Sex Pistols, TimeOut, 6 December. https://www.timeout.com/london/tv-reviews/never-mind-the-baubles-christmas-77-with-the-sex-pistols (accessed 25 September 2017). https://www.timeout.com/london/tv-reviews/never-mind-the-baubles-christmas-77-with-the-sex-pistols.

Here's the Artwork. 2017. www.herestheartwork.co.uk/viewContent.php?id=118 (accessed 9 August 2017).

Hutson, K. 2014. "Sex Pistols: Atlanta, Georgia—Full Concert," *YouTube*, https://www.youtube.com/watch?v=bzNMWp7wPmY (accessed 28 July 2018).

John Peel Wiki. http://peel.wikia.com/wiki/Sex_Pistols (accessed 6 May 2017).

Kris Needs. 2004. *trakMARX*, 17. www.trakmarx.com/2004_05/05_needs_f.htm (accessed 6 May 2017).

Les Dementlieu Punk Bibliotheque. www.dementlieu.com/~obik/ (accessed 29 July 2017).

Lloyd, P. A. 2016. "The Sex Pistols Anarchy Tour." *Bombed Out!* www.bombedoutpunk.com/history/photos-an-account-of-the-sex-pistols-anarchy-tour-in-1976 (accessed 6 May 2017).

Parker, 1976. "Sex Pistols and The Clash. Lanchester Polytechnic. 1976." *God Save The Sex Pistols* http://www.philjens.plus.com/pistols/pistols/Lanchester_Poly_live76.htm (accessed 28 July 2018).

Peter Don't Care. "Wolverhampton review," *Punk77*. www.punk77.co.uk/groups/sexpistolsrarephotos.htm (accessed 25 September 2017).

punk77. www.punk77.co.uk/groups/gobonyou.htm (accessed 19 June 2017).

punk77. Wolverhampton Lafayette Review. www.punk77.co.uk/groups/sexpistolsclublaf.htm (accessed 29 July 2017).

PunkyGibbon. "Angelic Upstarts Interview." http://punkygibbon.co.uk/bands/a/angelicupstarts_interview.html (accessed 25 September 2017).

Redstar73. 2006. "Interview with Mensi" (T. Mensforth).

Rock Portraits. https://rockportraits.wordpress.com/2014/10/02/the-sex-pistols/ (accessed 9 August 2017).

Scott, J. 2007. "Cake with Johnny Rotten." *The Guardian*, 20 July. www.theguardian.com/music/2007/jul/20/popandrock.sexpistols (accessed 25 September 2017).

———. 2015. "Worst Audience" for Punk Pistols, *The Star*, 26 September. www.thestar.co.uk/whats-on/gigs-and-music/worst-audience-for-punk-pistols-1-7479401 (accessed 29 July 2017).

Sex Pistols Official Website. "Anarchy in the U.K. 7"" 2018. http://www.sexpistolsofficial.com/records/anarchy-in-the-uk-7/ (accessed 28 July 2018).

Sex Pistols Official Website. "*Never Mind The Bollocks* Track by Track." 2017. http://www.sexpistolsofficial.com/nmtb-track-by-track/ (accessed 2 August 2017).

Sex Pistols Official Website. Sex Pistols Online Biography: http://www.sexpistolsofficial.com/bio/ (accessed 28 July 2018).

Super Seventies Rocksite! "Seventies Greatest Album Covers." www.superseventies.com/greatestalbumcovers.html (accessed 2 August 2017).

Tappijoe. 2012, "Peter Smith Personal Blog of Rock Concerts Attended. " https://vintage-rock.wordpress.com/2012/07/15/the-clash-white-riot-tour-newcastle-university-may-20th-1977/ (accessed 15 November 2015).

To the Left of West. "Account of Chelmsford Prison Gig." https://totheleftof-west.livejournal.com/6701.html (accessed 28 July 2018).

Whittaker, D. 2008. "The Boy Looked at Johnny." *BBC*. http://www.bbc.co.uk/leeds/content/articles/2008/10/08/music_david_whittaker_1976_feature.shtml (accessed 28 July 2018).

Williamson, D. 2016. "Anarchy in the UK: It's 40 Years Since a Single Heralded the Arrival of the Punk Revolution." *Wales Online*, November 26, 2016. www.walesonline.co.uk/news/politics/anarchy-uk-its-40-years-12231881 (accessed 3 September 2017).

INDEX

ABOUT THE AUTHOR

Peter Smith is emeritus professor of the University of Sunderland, UK. He has published more than three hundred articles and has written several textbooks. He is also a massive rock fan and has attended more than two thousand concerts. Peter is a big fan of the Sex Pistols and was lucky enough to see them at the height of their fame.